MW01026650

Praise for Michael E. Gerber, Brad Korn, and *The E-Myth Real Estate Agent*

Do you have a BIG vision and ambitious goals? Awesome! To succeed you'll need a system. Systems can ten times your business. Systems can make you a millionaire. Systems can give you freedom to do other things. **If you are looking for a system to be a great real estate agent, look no further: you've found it in *The E-Myth Real Estate Agent*.**

Stefan Swanepoel, international best-selling author of
20-plus books, including *Real Estate Trends Reports*

It is refreshing to hear an experienced real estate agent open up about the realities of the day-to-day real estate business. Most agents get into the business thinking they will have instant success and income, which is so untrue. Brad tells it like it is, and sets up anyone who implements his systems for success.

Rich Rector, chairman emeritus of Realty Executives International,
and co-author of *The E-Myth Real Estate Brokerage*

Brad Korn has created **a step-by-step blueprint for real estate agents who are looking to exponentially grow their businesses by utilizing cutting edge systems.** If you are an agent who wants to increase your income and create more time freedom for yourself then you have to read *The E-Myth Real Estate Agent*.

Than Merrill, author of the *The E-Myth Real Estate Investor*
and founder of FortuneBuilders.com

Did you know you have a successful real estate business in the making, one that can produce predictable results and one that you work on instead of just in? Have ever wondered what your scalable franchise-able models of success are? Have you ever tried to document them for others so that you get predictable results from your business? What are your "must execute" items each and every time you or someone on your team works with a client that wows the client? After reading this book, you should be able to answer with confidence those and other questions as you E-Myth your business into a business you own and are proud of rather than having a business that owns you.

Glenn Sanford, founder of eXp Realty and CEO and
chairman of the board of eXp World Holdings, Inc.

In a world filled with shiny objects, Brad has laid out the foolproof, simple system for any real estate agent to increase their production and serve more people in their communities. **This is a must-read-and-apply book for any agent who wants more from life and their business!**

Tim Davis, founder of Personal Branding Mastery™
and Agent Marketing Academy

Brad Korn is a leading authority at teaching real estate agents how to maximize their database to take them to the next level. **I've seen him practice what he preaches, teach what he practices, and the difference it makes in the businesses he impacts. The systems he shares are so simple anyone can make it in the real estate business if they apply what he shares.**

Hoss Pratt, author and creator, *The Listing Boss*

Do you want to save yourself stress, time, energy, and money? If so, read *The E-Myth Real Estate Agent*. Michael Gerber and Brad Korn get it. And they got it right with *The E-Myth Real Estate Agent*. As author of 7L, the 7L Referral System is a system of systems because of the wisdom of E-Myth. **You need a business that is consistent, repeatable, automated, and proactive. You need to start by reading this book.**

Michael Maher, author, *7L*

Brad Korn has cracked the puzzle of how to turn people you meet in your daily business into not only clients but raving fans who will jump hurdles to refer business to you. Our team spent two days with Brad, and when we arrived back to our business we had a fully set-up, organized and customized, automated real estate system. He set up the system, added the custom content, showed us how to make it work, and helped us to identify and bypass the issues that typically cause sales people to give up.

Lindsay and Wendy Smith,
real estate agents, Ontario, Canada

We wanted to share our result after one year of full implementation of Brad Korn's real estate systems. **By investing time in building some simple key systems and automating the follow-up process, then performing the money-making task only, I've been able to grow my business from a little over $1 million a year to $6.3 million in sold volume in just twelve months.** Since we invested in coaching and training along with following the model, new doors of opportunity to serve and grow ourselves as successful businesspeople have opened up. Brad is one of those people we have met who has been life-changing for us!

Shaun and Christina Rampersad, real estate agents, Orlando, FL

As a single dad and a rainmaker for my real estate team, there is a lot of stress in my life. The systems I've learned from Brad Korn have given me back my life. And have doubled and then doubled again my Gross Commission Income over the last few years. I've practiced the systems of Brad Korn in person and they have made me a successful real estate agent. My personal life and the business life of The Pikoff Team-Keller Williams Houston Preferred are all about systems. I ran a busy business in the past and would spin out of control, micromanage, and be working real estate every hour of the day. When I don't embrace those systems and just do real estate "naturally," my personal life and business can turn into a tornado. The up-and-down roller-coaster income pressures and the stress of being the best father for my children can make me physically ill. **Systems give me control and direction; and when I follow them and stay plugged in, I grow as a person and I make more money, and more importantly, I live a bigger and better life and enjoy my children.** I attend more soccer games with my son, Harrison, and more choir concerts with my daughter, Lexi. Brad Korn's systems have literally saved my life and given me a massive business that can be consistent and predictable!

Andrew Pikoff, J.D., LL.M., real estate agent, Houston, TX

I have known and worked alongside Brad Korn for more than a decade. **His commitment to developing world-class systems and then implementing them has always been his secret weapon.** Very few Realtors® can produce one hundred-plus transactions a year for over twenty years on autopilot, but Brad has. Whether real estate has been in a boom or bust cycle, Brad has always known at the start of each new year that one hundred-plus transactions would be in his pipeline. The ultimate proof that his systems work was in 2015 when his wife suffered a tragic brain injury and Brad stayed by her side day and night for almost six months before her passing, and his team of "one" brand new person followed the system and still sold ninety-eight homes. If you want the real secrets to long-term success in real estate, you will find them in the pages of this book.

Timothy Chin, CEO and founder, Referral Leaders International

Michael Gerber's *The E-Myth* is one of only four books I recommend as required reading. **For those looking to start and build a business of their own, this is the man who has coached more successful entrepreneurs than the next ten gurus combined.**

Timothy Ferris, #1 New York Times
best-selling author, *The 4-Hour Workweek*

Everyone needs a mentor, someone who tells it like it is, holds you accountable, and shows you your good, bad, and ugly. For millions of small business owners, Michael Gerber is that person. Let Michael be your mentor and you are in for a kick in the pants, the ride of a lifetime.

John Jantsch, author, *Duct Tape Marketing*

Michael Gerber is a master instructor and a leader's leader. As a combat F15 fighter pilot, I had to navigate complex missions with life-and-death consequences, but until I read *The E-Myth* and met Michael Gerber, my transition to the world of small business was a nightmare with no real flight plan. **The hands-on, practical magic of Michael's turnkey systems magnified by the raw power of his keen insight and wisdom have changed my life forever.**

Steve Olds, CEO, Stratworx.com

Michael Gerber's strategies in *The E-Myth* were instrumental in building my company from two employees to a global organization; I can't wait to see how applying the strategies from *Awakening the Entrepreneur Within* will affect its growth!

Dr. Ivan Misner, founder and chairman, BNI; author, *Masters of Sales*

Michael Gerber's gift to isolate the issues and present simple, direct, business-changing solutions shines bright with *Awakening the Entrepreneur Within*. **If you're interested in developing an entrepreneurial vision and plan that inspires others to action, buy this book, read it, and apply the processes Gerber brilliantly defines.**

Tim Templeton, author, *The Referral of a Lifetime*

Michael Gerber truly, truly understands what it takes to be a successful practicing entrepreneur and business owner. He has demonstrated to me over six years of working with him that for those who stay the course and learn much more than just "how to work on their business and not in it" then they will reap rich rewards. **I finally franchised my business, and the key to unlocking this kind of potential in any business is the teachings of Michael's work.**

Chris Owen, marketing director, Royal Armouries (International) PLC

Michael's work has been an inspiration to us. His books have helped us get free from the out-of-control life that we once had. His no-nonsense approach kept us focused on our ultimate aim rather than day-to-day stresses. He has helped take our business to levels we couldn't have imagined possible. In the Dreaming Room™ made us totally re-evaluate how we thought about our business and our life. We have now redesigned our life so we can manifest the dreams we unearthed in Michael's Dreaming Room™.

Jo and Steve Davison, founders, The Spinal Health Clinic Chiropractic Group and www.your-dream-life.com

Michael Gerber is an outrageous revolutionary who is changing the way the world does business. **He dares you to commit to your grandest dreams and then shows you how to make the impossible a reality. If you let him, this man will change your life.**

Fiona Fallon, founder, Divine and The Bottom Line

Michael Gerber is a genius. Every successful business person I meet has read Michael Gerber, refers to Michael Gerber, and lives by his words. You just can't get enough of Michael Gerber. **He has the innate (and rare) ability to tap into one's soul, look deeply, and tell you what you need to hear. And then, he inspires you, equips you with the tools to get it done.**

Pauline O'Malley, CEO, TheRevenueBuilder

When asked "Who was the most influential person in your life?" I am one of the thousands who don't hesitate to say "Michael E. Gerber." **Michael helped transform me from someone dreaming of retirement to someone dreaming of working until age one hundred.** This awakening is the predictable outcome of anyone reading Michael's new book.

Thomas O. Bardeen

Michael Gerber is an incredible business philosopher, guru, perhaps even a seer. He has an amazing intuition, which allows him to see in an instant what everybody else is missing; he sees opportunity everywhere. **While in the Dreaming Room™, Michael gave me the gift of seeing through the eyes of an awakened entrepreneur, and instantly my business changed from a regional success to serving clients on four continents.**

Keith G. Schiehl, president, Rent-a-Geek Computer Servi

Michael Gerber is among the very few who truly understand entrepreneurship and small business. While others talk about these topics in the form of theories, methodologies, processes, and so on, Michael goes to the heart of the issues. **Whenever Michael writes about entrepreneurship, soak it in as it is not only good for your business, but great for your soul.** His words will help you to keep your passion and balance while sailing through the uncertain sea of entrepreneurship.

Raymond Yeh, co-author, *The Art of Business*

Michael Gerber forced me to think big, think real, and gave me the support network to make it happen. A new wave of entrepreneurs is rising, much in thanks to his amazing efforts and very practical approach to doing business.

Christian Kessner, founder, Higher Ground Retreats and Events

Michael's understanding of entrepreneurship and small business management has been a difference maker for countless businesses, including Infusion Software. **His insights into the entrepreneurial process of building a business are a must-read for every small business owner.** The vision, clarity, and leadership that came out of our Dreaming Room™ experience were just what our company needed to recognize our potential and motivate the whole company to achieve it.

Clate Mask, president & CEO,
Infusion Software

Michael Gerber is a truly remarkable man. His steady openness of mind and ability to get to the deeper level continues to be an inspiration and encouragement to me. **He seems to always ask that one question that forces the new perspective break open and he approaches the new coming method in a fearless way.**

Rabbi Levi Cunin, Chabad of Malibu

The Dreaming Room™ experience was literally life-changing for us. **Within months, we were able to start our foundation and make several television appearances owing to his teachings.** He has an incredible charisma, which is priceless, but above all Michael Gerber awakens passion from within, enabling you to take action with dramatic results . . . starting today!

Shona and Shaun Carcary,
Trinity Property Investments Inc.
Home Vestors franchises

I thought E-Myth was an awkward name! What could this book do for me? **But when I finally got to reading it . . . it was what I was looking for all along.** Then, to top it off, I took a twenty-seven-hour trip to San Diego just to attend the Dreaming Room™, where Michael touched my heart, my mind, and my soul.

Helmi Natto, president,
Eye 2 Eye Optics, Saudi Arabia

I attended In the Dreaming Room™ and was challenged by Michael Gerber to "Go out and do what's impossible." So I did; **I became an author and international speaker and used Michael's principles to create a world-class company that will change and save lives all over the world.**

Dr. Don Kennedy, MBA; author, *5 AM & Already Behind*, www.bahbits.com

The E Myth

Real Estate Agent

*Why Most Real Estate
Businesses Don't Work
and What to Do About It*

MICHAEL E. GERBER

BRAD KORN

PRODIGY
BUSINESS BOOKS

Published by
Prodigy Business Books, Inc., Carlsbad, California.

Production Team
Patricia Beaulieu, COO, Prodigy Business Books, Inc.; Eve Gumpel, editor,
Good Writing Matters; Erich Broesel, cover designer, BroeselDesign, Inc.;
Nancy Ratkiewich, book production, njr productions; Jeff Kassebaum,
Michael E. Gerber author photographer, Jeff Kassebaum and Co.;
Angie Weston, Brad Korn co-author photographer, KC Moonlight Production.

For general information on other products and services, please visit the website:
www.MichaelEGerberCompanies.com

ISBN 978-1-61835-043-5 (cloth)
ISBN 978-1-61835-044-2 (audio)
ISBN 978-1-61835-005-3 (ebook)

Printed in the United States of America

10 9 8 7 6 5 4 3 2 1

To Luz Delia, my partner, my wife, my inspiration, and my life . . .
Thank you for your perseverance, your indomitable will,
And your kind and generous soul . . .
You're spectacular!

—Michael E. Gerber

I dedicate this book to Sonya, who always touched everyone she met
in a special way! She would make you feel like she had known you
forever. She was a giver, and in this book we both give you our
20-plus years of systems that allowed us to live an amazing life
and help me make her dreams come true to the very end,
as she ascended to return to her angels in 2015.

—Brad Korn

A SPECIAL MESSAGE
FROM BRAD AND MICHAEL

FROM BRAD:

Sometimes Your Business Has to Run Itself

This book has been in the making for over twenty-five years and the story you are about to read or listen to has given me an incredible business and income that has allowed me to provide for my family and given them, and me, a life I am proud of.

Unfortunately, it comes with the ultimate price! I started implementing the E-Myth into my business over twenty years ago at the writing of this book. However, Michael and I would not have crossed paths and written this book if it had not been for a series of events that started with a car accident on Friday, March 13th, 2015.

My wife, Sonya Korn, was on her way to pick up one of our elderly real estate clients to take her to a closing on her property that day. Unfortunately, Sonya never made it to our client's home. On the drive to pick her up, Sonya was clipped (so we think) on an entrance ramp of a busy highway. She was spun around 180 degrees and took a head-on collision in her Nissan Juke (a very small car). That impact caused the dash to push her femur through her hip socket and shatter her hip. The good news is the car did what it was supposed to do. It kept her alive.

Sonya had hip surgery the next morning which led to a twelve-week recovery time. The recovery was hard on her since she was so full of life and energy, and the doctor told her she could not put any weight on her hip for twelve weeks. This required her to sit a lot and not be active.

She made it through the recovery time. Twelve weeks after the accident (it was the first week of June), she was completely off crutches. Two weeks later, on June 23, 2015, after fully recovering, she was sleeping – only something wasn't right. She had been having some sleep issues since the accident and on that morning, she appeared to be in a deep sleep. She was snoring like she has never snored before. It was about 10:30 am and she still hadn't woken up. My daughter and I were concerned. We checked on her and she wouldn't respond to our attempts to wake her up. We immediately called 911.

Paramedics arrived quickly and got her stabilized in our bedroom. Everything seemed like it was going as well as it could as they prepared to take her to the emergency room. All of my daughters were at the house by the time they were ready to take her to the ER. We all went to the car to follow the ambulance. We sat in the driveway for about ten minutes. Finally, the ambulance took off and we followed. As I approached the paramedic at the ER doors, I asked if the ride went OK, not thinking for a moment that there would be anything to worry about. He looked at me like he had seen a ghost.

The paramedics had lost her on the way to the hospital for about four minutes, and the ER lost her for another four minutes or so. The lack of oxygen to her brain for that amount of time caused an anoxic (oxygen deprivation) brain injury. Monday, June 22, 2015 would be the last night any of us would hear Sonya's voice. The hospital immediately proceeded with standard medical practice, a medically induced coma, to stop any further brain damage – only we would not get her back. She was in a coma for the next five months.

I wanted to be certain we did everything we could to get her back. The next five months entailed taking her to several different specialists. One stop was one of the country's top brain injury specialists in Lincoln, Nebraska (about three hours from Kansas City). She was there for the next four or five months. But we would not get Sonya back. November 4, 2015, is the day we lost Sonya forever.

January of 2016 I was sitting in my office reflecting on memories of Sonya and thinking that I had been completely out of my business in Lincoln the entire five months that Sonya was in a coma. Yet we sold ninety-seven homes with only two members of our real estate team. Our system had carried them through while I was away from the day-to-day operations. It was at that moment I noticed *The E-Myth Revisited* book sitting on my bookshelf. I immediately googled "Michael Gerber" and found a phone number. I called and got voice mail. This was the message I left: "Mr. Gerber, you don't know me, but I implemented your book about twenty years ago and I wanted to thank you for giving me the last five months with my wife, who was in a coma. While I was at her side every day, three hours away from Kansas City, where I live, my real estate business sold ninety-seven homes with only two people on my team; our assistant, who had been with us about a year and one buyer's agent who had been with us only a few months. Thank you so much for sharing *The E-Myth* and giving me that time with my wife."

I had helped hundreds of the top real estate professionals across the globe. I had also worked with hundreds of the top loan officers just a few years prior. Michael asked me if I would write the book, *The E-Myth Real Estate Agent.*

I have put E-Myth into practice in my business for over twenty years and I have perfected and simplified the systems so that anyone can get the same results. The message I hope to convey and what I hope this book will do for you is challenge you to get out of your comfort zone. I realize it's comfortable to be there. I have been comfortable many times and luckily someone pushed me outside of my comfort zone, again. While I was out of my business for five months, the one thing I never thought about was if my bills were getting paid back at home in Kansas City. They were because the systems I had created 20 years prior were working to keep my business running even though I wasn't there.

Bad things will happen. If not to you, to someone close to you. When that "something" happens and you are in your comfort zone, it can suck you down to the uncomfortable real quick. The last thing you should have to worry about is "stuff" like your house payments or car payments being missed while you are supporting your family member or friend. So I am asking you today, do you have the WILL to get out of your comfort zone and stay well above your comfort zone? You will be glad you did when something bad comes your way.

FROM MICHAEL:

The Will & The Way

If you are a real estate agent and you have the WILL, this book is the WAY to produce 100-plus property sales per year, and it works every single time. There is no doubt about it; there is no talent it takes that is unique. What it requires is the WILL to literally produce 100 home sales per year.

Now there's got to be a reason why you're going to do that, beyond just the money of it, and the reason for doing that is absolutely CRITICAL! It's called the WHY. If you've got the WILL and you know your WHY, we have the WAY to produce this result every single time for every single one of you who read this book and listened to this book. No matter where you are in your career, no matter what you think you know, no matter what you have been doing, no matter what you think you should be doing. It's as mechanical as anything ever could possibly be.

The problem is everyone is making it more than what it is. Everybody's making it MORE complicated. Everybody's making it MORE sophisticated. Everybody's making it more than what, in fact, it really is.

It's a mechanical exercise.

It's a ritual.

It's DAILY.

It's like getting up and doing breathing exercises. It's like brushing your teeth regularly or showering regularly the way you do every single day. It's REGULAR, REGULAR, REGULAR.

And, in fact, it was built for a regular, ordinary human being to produce extraordinary results. So, the question is, "Are you ready to learn the WAY?" and the real question is, "Do you have the WILL to do it?

If your answer is YES, then Brad and I will take you through a regimen. AND this is not coaching. It is training, and I will train you how to do what you HAVE to do every single day. Not just Monday, Wednesday, and Friday . . . EVERY SINGLE DAY!

It's a ritual.

It's a ritual like yoga. It's a ritual like what the U.S. Navy Seals learn. It's a ritual like breathing. It is literally as ritual and fundamental as anything anyone has ever done or will ever do to become a master of anything.

In defense of being ordinary, I created an extraordinary system I could use to produce consistent results my entire life, every day —and the results are astonishing!

Can you imagine if every real estate agent stepped up and said, "I've got the WILL," and they just did the WAY! We're going to hold you accountable to it. Why are we going to hold you to it? Because you won't! Why won't you? Because you don't have the WILL, you just say you do.

On Tuesday, you're not going to want to do this.

On Thursday, you're going to forget I even spoke to you about this.

On Friday, you're going to be on to something else you think is better or sounds cool.

It is because you are wandering, wandering, wandering, wandering. You must come home to roost and anchor yourself. This is elemental. It's an economy of one. It's a company of one. It's what being a real estate agent is, but you realize this book is just the first step for a change. The first step for predictability. Without that first step, there is no future, other than a dismal one of never ever, ever, ever rising to the occasion.

Now, are you going to commit yourself to never ever, ever, ever rising to the occasion? Or are you going to commit yourself to literally becoming a STAR! A master of a system that works EVERY SINGLE time?

Which will it be?

CONTENTS

A WORD ABOUT THIS BOOK

Michael E. Gerber

My first E-Myth book was published in 1986. It was called *The E-Myth: Why Most Small Businesses Don't Work and What to Do About It*. Since that book, and the company I created to provide business development services to its many readers, millions have read *The E-Myth* and the book that followed it called *The E-Myth Revisited*, and tens of thousands have participated in our E-Myth Mastery programs.

The co-author of this book, Brad Korn, is one of my more enthusiastic readers, and as a direct result of his enthusiasm, his real estate business became one of our clients. He became, over the years, one of my friends.

This book is two things: the product of my lifelong work conceiving, developing, and growing the E-Myth way into a business model that has been applied to every imaginable kind of company in the world, as well as a product of Brad's extraordinary experience and success applying the E-Myth to the development of his equally extraordinary enterprise, Brad Korn, Coach Korn.

So it was that one day, while sitting with my muse, which I think of as my inner voice (and which many who know me think of as "here he goes again!"), I thought about the creation of an entire series of E-Myth Expert books. That series, including this book, would be co-authored by experts in every industry who had successfully applied my E-Myth principles to the extreme development of a sole proprietorship—an employer plus one—with the intent of growing it nationwide and even worldwide, which is what Brad had in mind as he began to discover the almost infinite range of opportunities provided by thinking the E-Myth way.

Upon seeing the possibilities of this new idea, I immediately invited co-authors such as Brad to join me. They said, "Let's do it!" and so we did.

Welcome to *The E-Myth Real Estate Agent: Why Most Real Estate Businesses Don't Work and What to Do About It.*

Read it, enjoy it, and let us—Brad and me—help you apply the E-Myth to the re-creation, development, and extreme growth of your real estate business into an enterprise you can be justifiably proud of.

To your life, your wisdom, and the life and success of your clients, I wish you good reading.

—Michael E. Gerber
Co-Founder | Chairman
Michael E. Gerber Companies, Inc.
Carlsbad, California

A NOTE FROM BRAD

Brad Korn

I was surprised in the beginning days of my career in the real estate industry that I was not given everything I needed to know to be successful in real estate. Now, more than twenty-five years later, as I write this book and reflect on the success I have had, I have learned one thing: if I had been told everything I thought I needed to know, it would not have not been the right information. It was not the information I will share with you in this book. I found this information in the E-Myth books, and I am bringing you more than twenty-five years of implementing, doing it wrong, and practicing what I wish I would have known when I first got into the real estate profession.

Real estate schools teach us what we need to know to get our real estate license. Once we pass the exam and get into the real world, the real estate industry teaches us, from day one, to go find the next deal. Agents are bombarded with the opportunity for fast-growth tools and products. Most providers strive for their product or service to be hands-off, automatic, and the agents expect them to explode their business. When I finished real estate school, I spent thousands of dollars more than I anticipated to get up and running. My first real estate company was kind enough to give me free office space, free copies, just about free everything. The tradeoff for that free stuff was to give up a big portion of my commission from every sale.

What I learned in those first few years confirmed why more than 60 percent of agents get out of real estate within three to five years.

The reason? Most agents can't dig out of the hole they started in because it costs money to start a business, and they commit the dollars and spend those dollars as soon as a contract is accepted, not after the money is in the bank account. They will put things on credit cards, or buy things not thinking about the commission split structure they have. Once you pass the licensing test and become a licensed real estate professional, you still have thousands of dollars to put toward getting your license, joining all the required associations, gaining access to the Multiple Listing Service or services, and getting lockboxes and keys to access those lockboxes. All that must happen before you can even show a house.

Once you do all that, you still need to put together a marketing or business plan to let the world know you can sell real estate. Keep in mind, after all that, you don't get to keep 100 percent of the commissions; in fact, you may have less than 20 percent to 40 percent of your commission dollars left over from every sale to support your lifestyle and put back into your business. If you believe you are keeping more than that, you will soon find out you were wrong, or you don't spend any money on your business at all.

If you put your license with a real estate broker, that owner runs a business as well, and will get some portion of your commissions if the brokerage offers services to help you grow your business. If you become your own broker, you will need money to run your business. A sustainable business cannot operate without income: therefore, your broker or your brokerage business will need to take some portion of your commissions. Real estate agents will calculate the commission percentage on a sale, and in their mind, start spending that money on things before the contract is closed. They commit future dollars before the transaction closes—which means they haven't actually made the money yet—and doing it without a business plan to succeed is setting up for failure.

Since I got into real estate more than twemty five years ago, I have encountered just about every obstacle real estate agents face throughout their real estate career. Including:

- Contractual understanding of complex real estate transactions and their hundreds of moving parts
- Understanding proven business success principles
- Getting the experience and training for masterful negotiating skills, marketing knowledge, and everything else it takes to run a successful real estate business

These challenges are critical parts of a real estate transaction, and not knowing these things can add up to a failed business. The industry statistics already confirm a better-than-60 percent chance real estate agents won't survive in this business.

Yes, I have experienced firsthand the struggles and failures most agents go through. However, I have also been blessed to experience tremendous success because I implemented the simple E-Myth principles in my real estate agent business early on. Because I have personally experienced so many failures and done the work myself, I can absolutely confirm that reading this book and implementing *The E-Myth Real Estate Agent* principles in your business will transform the results you can expect for your real estate business and how much more you can enjoy your life.

It has been more than two decades since I found Michael E. Gerber's book *The E-Myth: Why Most Small Businesses Don't Work and What to Do About It* and applied the systems to my business. Yet, I still remember like it was yesterday when I took my business from complete overwhelm and chaos to organized systems and began my journey to a successful real estate business that did not run my life, but gave me a great life to live and experience.

I was fortunate to have only been in business about five years when I began to implement the E-Myth principles. Many real estate agents, if they survive past the first three to five years, continue to sell the same number of homes year in and year out until they retire, or die. Because I created these systems early in my career, I can share my results with you in this book. At the time, five years into the real estate industry, my business was exploding. Yet, I wasn't making enough profit to hire more people. Unlike many of the real estate reality TV shows, where agents are making hundreds of thousands of dollars in commissions, the average commission in my market was closer to $4,000 to $5,000 per sale. Most real estate markets won't get you $10,000 to $30,000 on every sale.

The blessing in disguise was that I had to get more productivity from fewer people as I built my real estate team. That forced me to focus on systems that would deliver a predictable, consistent business from smaller commission checks. These systems also provided my clients an incredible customer experience, helping me capture more business and convert more prospects into clients with little effort. It also allowed me to create the systems that kept my small team accountable for the results most large teams and brokerages would see, and control our expenses to get the most profit possible from every transaction.

In the early days I was overwhelmed with everything coming at me day in and day out, and constantly reacting and having to resell myself to clients over and over. I had no time to work on my business. I was stuck on the typical roller-coaster ride at least 90 percent of real estate agents (even successful agents) find themselves on. I was struggling to consistently close one to two sales every month.

I attended a lot of conferences trying to find the secret to running a successful real estate business. I buried myself in more expenses, and more products and services promising huge results that never materialized. I continued to trade one idea for another, quit one product or website to use another. It doesn't take long to feel like you are inside a tornado and going nowhere. One month I was behind on the bills, and the next month I would catch up on all of them and feel like I had extra! Within a month or two, I was behind again.

The traditional way of running a real estate business had me working sixty-plus hours a week. I was missing out on things with my family. Those first three years ended up costing me my marriage because my real estate business was a family business. That was the moment I realized raising my three young girls on my own with a commission-only income was scarier than going through divorce.

My girls were one, two and five at the time. I knew I had to make this real estate thing work. Even with just a few years under my belt, I knew I couldn't keep our current lifestyle and raise my girls on a regular job working forty hours a week making $10 an hour. I had to figure this out. Real estate was my only option if I wanted control over my income and the lifestyle I wanted to provide for my girls.

That is about the time I found the E-Myth books and completely related to the business owner Michael talked about. I was going through the exact same issues being stuck in the technician role. The systems were so simple to understand, and I could see how to put my systems into action and create the turnkey systems. I share my systems with you in *The E-Myth Real Estate Agent*.

Over the past decade, I have shared the systems I created with thousands of real estate agents, and those who have started to put these systems into place are having life-changing and business-changing results. If these systems worked so predictably for me, they will work for you. You must implement these systems to get control of your real estate business too. The E-Myth Lead Generation, Lead Conversion and Client Fulfillment systems have been perfected over the past twenty-five years through my real estate business, to give every real estate agent the chance to have a business he or she can be proud of and be able to enjoy life again.

Keep in mind I have been running this one hundred-transaction real estate machine with approximately ten to fifteen hours of work each week. I have been able to share these systems across the globe and, now, write this book with Michael E. Gerber. If any agent working twenty to thirty hours a week implements these systems in their business, they could expect two to three times better results. *The E-Myth Real Estate Agent* makes real estate fun again. It takes very little effort to list and sell more real estate than 95 percent of the other agents in my market.

The E-Myth Real Estate Agent offers a simpler and more productive way of running a real estate business. The agents who understand it realize how simple it can be. When they trust the systems, they are able to focus on the one thing that will make every real estate business more profitable: feeding their database every day with new relationships. This first step is the one thing that will be most responsible for a successful, predictable real estate business. When you have raving fans and your business is growing naturally, it makes the whole thing fun again.

By personally applying the principles I outline in this book I have forced the real estate industry to take notice of my success. I am humbled to say that the E-Myth systems I implemented more than two decades ago are what made me a nationally recognized real estate agent. It still surprises me that with millions of real estate agents, a lil' ol' guy in Kansas City selling one hundred homes a year, with home sale prices hovering around $70,000 to $140,000 and a high end of $200,000 to $300,000, can figure out a predictable, profitable business model that doesn't require me to work sixty-plus hours a week. If I worked that many hours every week, this machine would be pumping out over 200 to 300 sales per year.

What I realized after connecting with Michael to write this book is that any real estate business—whether a solo agent starting on his or her own, or a team of 20, 200, or 2000 team members—the E-Myth principles work universally for any real estate-related business. Whether you are focused solely on new construction, resale, investment purchases for clients, selling bank assets, foreclosures, short sales, luxury homes, first-time homes, or property management, anyone can apply *The E-Myth Real Estate Agent* principles and achieve the same results I have. I have personally helped and watched a new agent who was about to get out of real estate create a team that had huge growth from a couple of hundred sales a year to more than 300- to 400-plus sales each year—and it was all done with the same, simple systems.

To truly benefit from this book, real estate agents need to stop looking for the easy, quick, hands-off distractions and, instead of focusing on the next deal, focus on the big picture and the long-term vision. This book will show you how to play the long game.

You can build a business that creates more income in less time instead of doing the daily grind and hustling for the next sale. The traditional ways of doing real estate will keep agents on the roller-coaster/hamster wheel and, as Michael says, you will be "doin' it, doin' it, doin' it" for years to come with no legacy or retirement in sight. The real estate business offers one of life's unlimited income potential opportunities. No other industry I am aware of can provide the flexibility, freedom, and more importantly, the income potential that anyone from any background can accomplish. There are no special skills required to follow the systems I share. If I could do it, anyone else can do the same.

The reality is, for most, being a real estate agent means long hours, the stress of an unpredictable income, and having to do things that are not fun for most people like: cold calling, knocking on doors, and all the other lead generation methods new real estate agents try. When most people get into real estate, they dream of making tens of thousands of dollars from every sale, and selling multiple homes every month with the chance to take control of their life and their schedule. *The E-Myth Real Estate Agent* is written to help change the fruitless hustle and make those dreams a reality.

Many years ago, I was blessed to find *The E-Myth* and was smart enough to read the entire book several times. I began to work on applying the systems and the principles that helped me support my three girls and give them an incredible life, full of all the opportunities and options many kids don't get. Today, with many years of experience as the real estate agent technician; transformational business leader; and internationally certified business coach, trainer and speaker, I now have the ultimate lifetime honor of co-authoring the book that will help you transform your real estate business into the dream you had when you started your real estate path. A true business that is systematized and profitable every year, and can survive in up-and-down markets without you being a slave to business or market conditions.

Start by simply clearing your head of everything you have been told about real estate. There is no easy way to get there, and there isn't any product or service that will instantly give you hundreds of sales every year. Open up your mind to a new way of thinking. Open your mind to accept the fact that it really can be this simple. I can only hope that this book will have a significant impact on you, like the original *E-Myth* had on me so many years ago.

—Brad Korn
REALTOR®, Speaker,
Trainer & Business Coach
Kansas City, Missouri
www.coachkorn.com

PREFACE

Michael E. Gerber

I am not a real estate agent, though I have helped dozens of real estate agents reinvent their real estate agencies over the past forty years.

I like to think of myself as a thinker, maybe even a dreamer. Yes, I like to *do* things. But before I jump in and get my hands dirty, I prefer to think through what I'm going to do and figure out the best way to do it. I imagine the impossible, dream big, and then try to figure out how the impossible can become the possible. After that, it's about how to turn the possible into reality.

Over the years, I've made it my business to study how things work and how people work—specifically, how things and people work best together to produce optimum results. That means creating an organization that can do great things and achieve more than any other organization can.

This book is about how to produce the best results as a real-world real estate agent in the development, expansion, and *liberation* of your business. In the process, you will come to understand what the practice of real estate—as a *business*—is and what it isn't. If you keep focusing on what it isn't, you're destined for failure. But if you turn your sights on what it is, the tide will turn.

This book, intentionally small, is about big ideas. The topics we'll discuss in this book are the very issues that real estate agents face daily in their companies. You know what they are: money, management, clients, and many more. My aim is to help you begin the exciting process of totally transforming the way you do business.

As such, I'm confident that *The E-Myth Real Estate Agent* could well be the most important book on the practice of real estate as a business that you'll ever read.

Unlike other books on the market, my goal is not to tell you how to do the work you do. Instead, I want to share with you the E-Myth philosophy as a way to revolutionize the way you think about the work you do. I'm convinced that this new way of thinking is something real estate agents everywhere must adopt in order for their real estate agencies to flourish during these trying times. I call it strategic thinking, as opposed to tactical thinking.

In strategic thinking, also called systems thinking, you, the real estate agent, will begin to think about your entire business—the broad scope of it—instead of focusing on its individual parts. You will begin to see the end game (perhaps for the first time) rather than just the day-to-day routine that's consuming you—the endless, draining work I call "doing it, doing it, doing it."

Understanding strategic thinking will enable you to create a company that becomes a successful business, with the potential to flourish as an even more successful enterprise. But in order for you to accomplish this, your company, your business, and certainly your enterprise must work *apart* from you instead of *because* of you.

The E-Myth philosophy defines a company as a sole proprietorship, a business, or an enterprise, so you will see these designations used throughout the book. In some industries, a company can also be called a practice. For the purposes of this book, my references to a "company" refer to a sole proprietorship.

Accordingly, a company is created and owned by a technician, a business is created and owned by a manager, and an enterprise is created and owned by an entrepreneur.

The E-Myth philosophy says that a highly successful real estate business can grow into a highly successful real estate business, which in turn can become the foundation for an inordinately successful real estate enterprise that runs smoothly and efficiently without the real estate agent having to be in the office for ten hours a day, six days a week.

So what is "the E-Myth," exactly? The E-Myth is short for the Entrepreneurial Myth, which says that most businesses fail to fulfill their potential because most people starting their own business are not entrepreneurs at all. They're actually what I call *technicians suffering from an entrepreneurial seizure*. When technicians suffering from an entrepreneurial seizure start a real estate business of their own, they almost always end up working themselves into a frenzy; their days are booked solid with appointments. These real estate agents are burning the candle at both ends, fueled by too much coffee and too little sleep. Most of the time, they can't even stop to think.

In short, the E-Myth says that most real estate agents don't own a true business—most own a job. They're doing it, doing it, doing it, hoping like hell to get some time off, but never figuring out how to get their business to run without them. And if your business doesn't run well without you, what happens when you can't be in two places at once? Ultimately, your company will fail.

There are a number of schools throughout the world dedicated to teaching the art of real estate. The problem is they fail to teach the *business* of it. And because no one is being taught how to run a company as a business, some real estate agents find themselves having to close their doors every year. You could be a world-class expert in securing listings and negotiating contracts, but when it comes to building a successful business, all that specified knowledge matters exactly zilch.

The good news is that you don't have to be among the statistics of failure in the real estate agent profession. The E-Myth philosophy I am about to share with you in this book has been successfully applied to thousands of real estate agencies just like yours with extraordinary results.

The key to transforming your company—and your life—is to grasp the profound difference between going to work on your business (systems thinker) and going to work in your business (tactical thinker). In other words, it's the difference between going to work on your business as an entrepreneur and going to work in your business as a real estate agent.

The two are not mutually exclusive. In fact, they are essential to each other. The problem with most real estate agencies is that the systems thinker—the entrepreneur—is completely absent. And so is the vision.

The E-Myth philosophy says that the key to transforming your company into a successful enterprise is knowing how to transform yourself from successful real estate agent into a successful technician-manager-entrepreneur. In the process, everything you do in your real estate business will be transformed. The door is then open to turning it into what it should be—a company, a business, and an enterprise of pure joy.

The E-Myth not only can work for you, it will work for you. In the process, it will give you an entirely new experience of your business and beyond.

To your future and your life. Good reading.

—Michael E. Gerber
Co-Founder | Chairman
Michael E. Gerber Companies, Inc.
Carlsbad, California

ACKNOWLEDGMENTS

Michael E. Gerber

As always, and never to be forgotten, there are those who give of themselves to make my work possible.

To my dearest and most forgiving partner, wife, friend, and co-founder, Luz Delia Gerber, whose love and commitment takes me to places I would often not go unaccompanied.

To Trish Beaulieu, wow, you are splendid.

To Eve Gumpel, my Eagle-eyed copyeditor, we couldn't have done it without your level of expertise and experience.

And to Nancy Ratkiewich, whose work has been essential for you who are reading this.

To those many, many dreamers, thinkers, storytellers, and leaders, whose travels with me In The Dreaming Room™ have given me life, breath, and pleasure unanticipated before we met. To those many participants in my life (you know who you are), thank you for taking me seriously, and joining me in this exhilarating quest.

And, of course, to my co-authors, all of you, your genius, wisdom, intelligence, and wit have supplied me with a grand view of the world, which would never have been the same without you.

Love to all.

AKNOWLEDGMENTS

Brad Korn

T he world is a crazy place, and human beings are a little crazy too. This life is a hard journey, and the old saying "Time reveals all" is true. Another saying that has stuck with me is, "In life 25 percent of the people you meet will love you, and they will take a bullet for you. Twenty-five percent of the people you know who love you can be convinced to doubt you, 25 percent of the people who don't necessarily trust you or like you can be persuaded to like you, and 25 percent of the people you meet will never like you and do anything to drag you down."

This section of the book is to the 25 percent who have loved me from the beginning and support me. And, to the 25 percent who still like me and haven't been persuaded not to like me (I also listed a few of the 25 percent who did like me, and have been persuaded not to like me.).

To the people who helped with getting this book launched by offering advice, direction, and encouragement: Michael E. Gerber, Stefan Swanepoel, Sam Miller, Tim Davis, Michael Maher, and Jay Papasan.

To my business and marketing coaches over the past twenty years: James Malinchak, Tony DiCello, Dianna Kokoszka, Cheiri Lowry, Ron Patulski, and Cleve Adams.

To my coaching clients who truly implemented ideas from every call. Through coaching we perfected systems to get results and create duplicable processes: Jeremy Forcier, Lindsay and Wendy Smith,

Andrew Pikoff, Blair Taylor, Amy and John Simmons, Susan and
Zander Oldendorp, Mike Lesmeister, Marlene Reyes, Bob O'Bryant,
Jim Blehm, Alivia Roberts, Jill Giese, Jay White, Michael Routh, Ann
Andre, Judy DeGreeff, Tyler Willmann, Amy Kite, Haro Setian, and
every coaching client I have ever had the pleasure of working with.
Also, for Timothy Chin for recruiting me to be a business coach back
in 2005. Without Timothy, I would have never thought to become a
coach to help others enjoy their life and business.

To my mentors in the real estate industry who helped me under-
stand the real estate business and encouraged me to build a successful
real estate machine: Howard Brinton, Allen Hainge, Dave Beason,
David Knox, Gary Keller, Joe Stumpf, Brian Buffini, Dave Jenks, David
Rogers, Dennis Curtin, Bonnie Hutchcroft, the CyberStars and Star
Power Real Estate Agents.

To my family and friends who have supported me and kept me
working hard to be a better person and to always push forward. First
and foremost, my wife of eighteen years, Sonya Korn, who never
gave up on me and always supported everything I did, whether she
wanted to go along with it or not, whom we all miss dearly every day.
To my daughters for being great kids and growing up to be women.
I am proud to call them my daughters: Lindsay, Allison, Elizabeth,
and Savannah. To my new life companion Lynette, and her tremendous children Erin, Colin, and Brennan for helping me get this book
completed and giving me the time to get through all the edits and
whom, I know, will support what follows the publishing of this book.

There are so many other people I did not specifically mention
who are very much a part of this book and responsible for the success
I have had. I would like to thank anyone that has impacted my life
and career that I did not mention here. You know who you are.

INTRODUCTION

Michael E. Gerber

As I write this book, the aftermath of the recession and the slow economic recovery continue to take their toll on American businesses. Like any other industry, real estate is not immune. Real estate agents all over the country are watching, as homebuyer budgets are tight and there's a lot of competition for a few good deals.

Faced with a struggling economy and waning prospects, many real estate agents I've met are asking themselves, "Why did I ever become a real estate agent in the first place?"

And it isn't just a money problem. After thirty-five years of working with small businesses, many of them real estate agencies, I'm convinced that the dissatisfaction experienced by countless real estate agents is not just about money. To be frank, the recession doesn't deserve all the blame, either. While the financial crisis our country faced certainly hasn't made things any better, the problem started long before the economy tanked. Let's dig a little deeper. Let's go back to school.

Can you remember that far back? Whichever university or college you attended, you probably had some great teachers who helped you become the fine real estate agent you are. These schools excel at teaching the facts about real estate; they'll teach you everything you need to know about APR, contracts, and the Multiple Listing Service. But what they *don't* teach is the consummate skill set needed to be a successful real estate agent, and they certainly don't teach what it takes to build a successful real estate enterprise.

Obviously, something is seriously wrong. The education that real estate professionals receive in school doesn't go far enough, deep enough, broad enough. Real estate programs don't teach you how to relate to the *enterprise* of real estate or to the business of real estate; they only teach you how to relate to the *practice* of real estate. In other words, they merely teach you how to be an *effective* rather than a *successful* real estate agent. Last time I checked, they weren't offering degrees in success. That's why most real estate agents are effective, but few are successful.

Although a successful real estate agent must be effective, an effective real estate agent does not have to be—and in most cases isn't—successful.

An effective real estate agent is capable of executing his or her duties with as much certainty and professionalism as possible.

A successful real estate agent, on the other hand, works balanced hours, has little stress, leads rich and rewarding relationships with friends and family, and has an economic life that is diverse, fulfilling, and shows a continuous return on investment.

A successful real estate agent finds time and ways to give back to the community but at little cost to his or her sense of ease.

A successful real estate agent is a leader, not simply someone who teaches novices real estate, but a sage: a rich person (in the broadest sense of the word); a strong father, mother, wife, or husband; a friend, teacher, mentor, and spiritually grounded human being; and a person who can see clearly into all aspects of what it means to lead a fulfilling life.

So let's go back to the original question. Why did you become a real estate agent? Were you striving to just be an effective one, or did you dream about real and resounding success?

I don't know how you've answered that question in the past, but I am confident that once you understand the strategic thinking laid out in this book, you will answer it differently in the future.

If the ideas here are going to be of value to you, it's critical that you begin to look at yourself in a different, more productive way. I am suggesting you go beyond the mere technical aspects of your daily job as a real estate agent and begin instead to think strategically about your real estate business as both a business and an enterprise.

I often say that most companies don't work—the people who own them do. In other words, most real estate agencies are jobs for the real estate agents who own them. Does this sound familiar? The real estate agent, overcome by an entrepreneurial seizure, has started his or her own company, become his or her own boss, and now works for a lunatic!

The result: the real estate agent is running out of time, patience, and ultimately, money. Not to mention paying the worst price anyone can pay for the inability to understand what a true company is, what a true business is, and what a true enterprise is—the price of his or her life.

In this book I'm going to make the case for why you should think differently about what you do and why you do it. It isn't just the future of your real estate business that hangs in the balance. It's the future of your life.

The E-Myth Real Estate Agent is an exciting departure from my sole-authored books. In this book, an expert—a successful real estate agent who has successfully applied the E-Myth principles to the development of his real estate business—is sharing his secrets about how he achieved extraordinary results using the E-Myth paradigm. In addition to the time-tested E-Myth strategies and systems I'll be sharing with you, you'll benefit from the wisdom, guidance, and practical tips provided by a legion of real estate agents who've been in your shoes.

The problems that afflict real estate agencies today don't only exist in the field of real estate; the same problems are confronting every organization of every size, in every industry, and in every country in the world. *The E-Myth Real Estate Agent* is next in a new series of E-Myth Expert books that will serve as a launching pad for Michael E. Gerber Partners™ to bring a legacy of expertise to small, struggling businesses in *all* industries. This series will offer an exciting opportunity to understand and apply the significance of E-Myth methodology in both theory and practice to businesses in need of development and growth.

The E-Myth says that only by conducting your *business* in a truly innovative and independent way will you ever realize the unmatched joy that comes from creating a truly independent business, a business that works *without* you rather than *because* of you.

The E-Myth says that it is only by learning the difference between the work of a *business* and the business of *work* that real estate agents will be freed from the predictable and often overwhelming tyranny of the unprofitable, unproductive routine that consumes them on a daily basis.

The E-Myth says that what will make the ultimate difference between the success or failure of your real estate business is first and foremost how you *think* about your business, as opposed to how hard you work in it.

So let's think it through together. Let's think about those things—work, clients, money, time—that dominate the world of real estate agents everywhere.

Let's talk about planning. About growth. About management. About getting a life!

Let's think about improving your and your family's life through the development of an extraordinary company. About getting the life you've always dreamed of but never thought you could actually have.

Envision the future you want, and the future is yours.

The Story of Steve
and Peggy

Michael E. Gerber

Make every detail perfect, and limit the number of details to perfect.
—Jack Dorsey, co-founder of Twitter

E very business is a family business. To ignore this truth is to court disaster.

This is true whether or not family members actually work in the business. Whatever their relationship with the business, every member of a real estate agent's family will be greatly affected by the decisions a real estate agent makes about the business. There's just no way around it.

Unfortunately, like most business people, real estate agents tend to compartmentalize their lives. They view their business as a profession—what they do—and therefore it's none of their family's business.

"This has nothing to do with you," says the real estate agent to his wife, with blind conviction. "I leave work at the office and family at home."

And with equal conviction, I say, "Not true!"

In actuality, your family and real estate business are inextricably linked to one another. What's happening in your company is also happening at home. Consider the following and ask yourself if each is true:

If you're angry at work, you're also angry at home.

If you're out of control at your real estate business, you're equally out of control at home.

If you're having trouble with money at your company, you're also having trouble with money at home.

If you have communication problems at your company, you're also having communication problems at home.

If you don't trust in your company, you don't trust at home.

If you're secretive at your company, you're equally secretive at home.

And you're paying a huge price for it!

The truth is that your company and your family are one—and you're the link. Or you should be. Because if you try to keep your company and your family apart, if your company and your family are strangers, you will effectively create two separate worlds that can never wholeheartedly serve each other. Two worlds that split each other apart.

Let me tell you the story of Steve and Peggy Walsh.

The Walshes met in college. They were partners in a study club for a finance class—Steve a real estate student and Peggy in business administration. When their discussions started to wander beyond market analysis and investment theory and into their personal lives, they discovered they had a lot in common. By the end of the course, they weren't just talking in class; they were talking on the phone every night . . . and not about finance.

Steve thought Peggy was absolutely brilliant, and Peggy considered Steve the most passionate man she knew. It wasn't long before they were engaged and planning their future together. A week after graduation, they were married in a lovely garden ceremony in Peggy's childhood home.

While Steve studied real estate at a local school, Peggy entered a business Master's program nearby. Over the next few years, the couple worked hard to keep their finances afloat. They worked long hours and studied constantly; they were often exhausted and struggled to make ends meet. But through it all, they were committed to what they were doing and to each other.

After graduating, Steve became an agent in a busy real estate business while Peggy began working in a large corporation nearby. Soon afterward, the couple had their first son, and Peggy decided to take some time off to be with him. Those were good years. Steve and Peggy loved each other very much, were active members in their church, participated in community organizations, and spent quality time together. The Walshes considered themselves one of the most fortunate families they knew.

But work became troublesome. Steve grew increasingly frustrated with the way the company was run. "I want to go into business for myself," he announced one night at the dinner table. "I want to start my own business."

Steve and Peggy spent many nights talking about the move. Was it something they could afford? Did Steve really have the skills necessary to make a real estate business a success? Were there enough clients and deals to go around? What impact would such a move have on Peggy's career at the local business, their lifestyle, their son, their relationship? They asked all the questions they thought they needed to answer before Steve went into business for himself . . . but they never really drew up a concrete plan.

Finally, tired of talking and confident that he could handle whatever he might face, Steve committed to starting his own real estate business. Because she loved and supported him, Peggy agreed, offering her own commitment to help in any way she could. So Steve quit his job, took out a second mortgage on their home, and leased a small office nearby.

In the beginning, things went well. A housing boom had hit the town, and new families were pouring into the area. Steve had no trouble getting new clients. His company expanded, quickly outgrowing his office.

Within a year, Steve had employed an office manager, Clarissa, to run the front desk and handle the administrative side of the business.

He also hired a bookkeeper, Tim, to handle the finances. Steve was ecstatic with the progress his young company had made. He celebrated by taking his wife and son on vacation to Italy.

Of course, managing a business was more complicated and time-consuming than working for someone else. Steve not only supervised all the jobs Clarissa and Tim did, but also was continually looking for work to keep everyone busy. When he wasn't scanning real estate websites to stay abreast of what was going on in the field or attending industry events to stay current, he was showing houses, wading through client paperwork, or speaking with the local Real Estate Commission. He also found himself spending more and more time on the telephone dealing with client complaints and nurturing relationships.

As the months went by and more and more clients came through the door, Steve had to spend even more time just trying to keep his head above water.

By the end of its second year, the business, now employing two full-time and two part-time people, had moved to a larger office downtown. The demands on Steve's time had grown with the company.

He began leaving home earlier in the morning and returning later at night. He drank more. He rarely saw his son anymore. For the most part, Steve was resigned to the problem. He saw the hard work as essential to building the "sweat equity" he had long heard about.

Money was also becoming a problem for Steve. Although the business was growing like crazy, money always seemed scarce when it was really needed.

When Steve had worked for somebody else, he had been paid twice a month. In his own company, he often had to wait—sometimes for months. Even if a property was in escrow, buyers and sellers sometimes could not come to terms, the buyer didn't qualify for mortgages, and deals fell through. Of course, no matter how slowly Steve got paid, he still had to pay *his* people. This became a relentless problem. Steve often felt like a juggler dancing on a tightrope. A fire burned in his stomach day and night.

To make matters worse, Steve began to feel that Peggy was insensitive to his troubles. Not that he often talked to his wife about the business. "Business is business" was Steve's mantra. "It's my responsibility to handle things at the office and Peggy's responsibility to take care of her own job and the family."

Peggy was working late hours at the corporation, and they'd brought in a nanny to help with their son. Steve couldn't help but notice that his wife seemed resentful, and her apparent lack of understanding baffled him. Didn't she see that he had a business to take care of? That he was doing it all for his family? Apparently not.

As time went on, Steve became even more consumed and frustrated by his company. When he went off on his own, he remembered saying, "I don't like people telling me what to do." But people were still telling him what to do.

Not surprisingly, Peggy grew more frustrated by her husband's lack of communication. She cut back on her own hours at her job to focus on their family, but her husband still never seemed to be around. Their relationship grew tense and strained. The rare moments they *were* together were more often than not peppered by long silences—a far cry from the heartfelt conversations that had characterized their relationship's early days, when they'd talk into the wee hours of the morning.

Meanwhile, Tim, the bookkeeper, was also becoming a problem for Steve. Tim never seemed to have the financial information Steve needed to make decisions about payroll, billing, and general operating expenses, let alone how much money was available for Steve and Peggy's living expenses.

When questioned, Tim would shift his gaze to his feet and say, "Listen, Steve, I've got a lot more to do around here than you can imagine. It'll take a little more time. Just don't press me, okay?"

Overwhelmed by his own work, Steve usually backed off. The last thing Steve wanted was to upset Tim and have to do the books himself. He could also empathize with what Tim was going through, given the company's growth over the past year.

Late at night in his office, Steve would sometimes recall his first years out of school. He missed the simple life he and his family had shared. Then, as quickly as the thoughts came, they would vanish. He had work to do and no time for daydreaming. "Having my own company is a great thing," he would remind himself. "I simply have to apply myself, as I did in school, and get on with the job. I have to work as hard as I always have when something needed to get done."

Steve began to live most of his life inside his head. He began to distrust his people. They never seemed to work hard enough or to care about his company as much as he did. If he wanted to get something done, he usually had to do it himself.

Then one day, the office manager, Clarissa, quit in a huff, frustrated by the amount of work that her boss was demanding of her. Steve was left with a desk full of papers and a telephone that wouldn't stop ringing.

Clueless about the work Clarissa had done, Steve was overwhelmed by having to pick up the pieces of a job he didn't understand. His world turned upside down. He felt like a stranger in his own company.

Why had he been such a fool? Why hadn't he taken the time to learn what Clarissa did in the office? Why had he waited until now?

Ever the trouper, Steve plowed into Clarissa's job with everything he could muster. What he found shocked him. Clarissa's work space was a disaster area! Her desk drawers were a jumble of papers, coins, pens, pencils, rubber bands, envelopes, business cards, fee slips, eye drops, and candy.

"What was she thinking?" Steve raged.

When he got home that night, even later than usual, he got into a shouting match with Peggy. He settled it by storming out of the house to get a drink. Didn't anybody understand him? Didn't anybody care what he was going through?

He returned home only when he was sure Peggy was asleep. He slept on the couch and left early in the morning, before anyone was awake. He was in no mood for questions or arguments. When Steve got to his office the next morning, he immediately headed for the break room, where he could put his head down to soothe his throbbing headache.

What lessons can we draw from Steve and Peggy's story? I've said it once and I'll say it again: *Every business is a family business*. Your business profoundly touches all members of your family, even if they never set foot inside your office. Every business either gives to the family or takes from the family, just as individual family members do.

If the business takes more than it gives, the family is always the first to pay the price.

In order for Steve to free himself from the prison he created, he would first have to admit his vulnerability. He would have to confess to himself and his family that he really didn't know enough about his own business and how to grow it.

Steve tried to do it all himself. Had he succeeded, had the business supported his family in the style he imagined, he would have burst with pride. Instead, Steve unwittingly isolated himself, thereby achieving the exact opposite of what he sought.

He destroyed his life—and his family's life along with it.

Repeat after me: *Every business is a family business.*

Are you like Steve? I believe that all real estate agents share a common soul with him. You must learn that a business is only a business. It is not your life. But it is also true that your business can have a profoundly negative impact on your life unless you learn how to do it differently than most real estate agents do it—and definitely differently than Steve did it.

Steve's real estate business could have served his and his family's life. But for that to happen, he would have had to learn how to master his business in a way that was completely foreign to him.

Instead, Steve's business consumed him. Because he lacked a true understanding of the essential strategic thinking that would have allowed him to create something unique, Steve and his family were doomed from day one.

This book contains the secrets that Steve should have known. If you follow in Steve's footsteps, prepare to have your life and business fall apart. But if you apply the principles we'll discuss here, you can avoid a similar fate.

Let's start with the subject of *money*. But, before we do, let's read the real estate agent's view about the story I just told you. Let's talk about Brad's journey . . . and yours. ✤

A Typical Real Estate Agent's Story

Brad Korn

The difference between great people and everyone else is that great people create their lives actively, while everyone else is created by their lives, passively waiting to see where life takes them next. The difference between the two is the difference between living fully and just existing.
—Michael E. Gerber

I spent my first three years in real estate spinning my wheels, working two other jobs, spending my commission checks before the transactions closed, hiring team members before I was ready for them, and continuing to spend money faster than I was making it. That ultimately led to a bankruptcy—all before I had hit my fourth year in real estate.

Part of the problem is the way real estate agents receive money. For me, it was always great to get a BIG check every time a house sold. I had never received paychecks of $5,000 or $10,000 before. My problem was, whenever big checks like that were coming in, I had that money committed and spent by the time I received the check. I was always trying to catch up with bills and everything else because the income was coming in like a roller-coaster ride. It was very unpredictable.

I did all the things I was told to do when cold calling, meeting and networking, targeting neighborhoods, etc. All this work still didn't bring in the cash fast enough. I would fall behind one month and catch up the next. I was not running my real estate practice like a business. I was just dumping everything into my personal checking account and spending it as I needed it, hoping there was enough in there to pay for everything. Most of the time, I needed more than I had in the account

Like anything, real estate is truly about doing it consistently and daily over a long period of time. I wasn't going to give up. I saw the potential in real estate to support my girls as they grew up, get them through college . . . and oh yes, did I mention FOUR weddings? Whew! I did whatever it took to keep my real estate habit going.

The E-Myth books explain why small-business people get consumed with their job/business. It happens because so many of us are, as Michael describes, technicians. Most people who get their real estate license start, and get stuck, in the technician role their entire career. The real estate business can take control of your life. You can find yourself "doing real estate" all the time—literally morning, noon, and night. Without a plan, the real estate business can, and will, run your life.

Those beginning in real estate are working it as much as they can to get that very first commission check. Once they get those first sales under their belt, the majority go into survival mode, working hard to get a consistent flow of income. The worst thing that can happen is that you end up loving what you do and do not perceive real estate activities as work. For many, showing houses can be fun. Writing a contract on a $500,000 house is ALWAYS fun! Spending that paycheck when the sale closes is the most fun.

The reality, especially when we are new to real estate or have not created a consistent flow of income from real estate, is that if there is a slight opportunity to "make money," we will drop everything else in our life to make that deal happen. Some will even be late to, or miss, a child's sporting event or a family member's birthday if someone wants to see a million-dollar property! And yet, it can take months to cash in on the deal.

Every Business Is a Family Business

Michael says that every business is a family business. The real estate business can be an all-the-time, every-day business. Whether you believe you are in a family business or not, you are. Your family is technically "in" the real estate business with you when it controls your life. In fact, in real estate, you will hear agents say, and maybe even say yourself, "Real estate IS my life." A national commercial on TV once told consumers, "Real estate is our life."

Real estate is a business that takes place any time of the day or week. I did not have the conversations with my family to let them know what making a lot of money in real estate would require.

As a result, in my early days in real estate, my family suffered. In fact, I had to keep two other jobs to support my real estate habit. I was "practicing" real estate and working other hourly jobs to make real money that would pay our bills. I was working all the time and planning my work schedule around my spouse's schedule. I thought we were working smart and becoming a successful family, moving toward a wonderful life.

Families are stronger when they spend time together, love each other, and support each other. I felt like I was connected in my family situation. I never felt like I was missing our children's activities. I felt like we were all connected as a family. What I didn't realize is that every minute of every day I was thinking real estate, and I wasn't in tune with my family like I thought I was. I was young and wanted to be successful, provide for my family, and live in a big house with fancy cars. Because my mind was always on real estate, I was "checked out" more than I thought.

That workaholic attitude eventually affected all of us for a lifetime and led to divorce. The scary thing was that I didn't see it coming.

I thought we were the perfect family. When I look back and reflect on it, I guess I see why the situations that led to divorce happened. Doesn't mean I agree, but that doesn't really matter now, does it? We still got divorced.

I found myself a single dad with three little girls and a commission-only job that hadn't paid me more than $10,000 that past year. I had only been working minimum-wage jobs part-time since I started selling real estate three years prior. Now I was forced to make this "real estate thing" work. This life lesson is one reason I am sharing this book with you.

Starting All Over

The best thing that happened was moving back to Kansas City in 1995 just after our third daughter was born. Getting back to Kansas City was a critical part of my success and led to my writing *The E-Myth Real Estate Agent* with Michael E. Gerber. In Minneapolis, I knew NO ONE, and I do mean NO ONE. I did not have a list of one hundred people to call when I got started in real estate. I had to contact total strangers to get any business at all.

Moving back to Kansas City meant starting all over again.

I was a technician again, only I didn't know what a "technician" was since I hadn't read *The E-Myth* yet. I was putting the sweat equity into doin' it, doin' it, doin' it every day; only this time, I was a single father trying to raise three girls on a commission-only business.

The difference is, I was now aware of the real deal that real estate is no different than a brick-and-mortar business. If you open a store in the back alley and people don't know you are there, you will go out of business. Most real estate agents do exactly what I did. I sent out an "announcement card" and expected everyone who knew me to pick up the phone and start buying and selling homes. I was repeating the first three years all over again.

How many people are going to remember that business in the back alley if they only get ONE postcard or invite? When people wake up every day, the first thing on their mind is not "I need to help Brad grow his real estate business."

To be successful in real estate I had to get in front of people. Make calls every day. I held open houses when I had someone to watch my girls or when they were with their mother. I was still mailing out things and continuing to get a painfully low return on my investment. I did what it took to make it work. I took the girls to showings with me, to open houses with me, and they basically lived in my car with me while I was working to really get this thing off the ground. Over the course of a year I went from zero sales to about $1 million in sales volume. All that hard work paid off!

Think so? You'd be wrong!

A million-dollar producer in real estate it probably making less than $20,000 a year in income.

I will share more in another chapter about the turnkey system that will change your real estate business forever. It will automate your real estate business and truly make the phone ring again.

The 'Get the Next Deal' Treadmill

The industry has taught us from day one of our career to call, mail, email or market until we get the next deal. It's no wonder the real estate industry has a failure rate of over 60 percent in the first two to three years. The entire industry revolves around getting the next deal. That's another one of the things wrong with our industry—the need for fast money, and lots of it.

New agents typically try to generate business by picking up the phone and making calls. When cold calling for business, you are advised to keep calling until you get the next appointment. If you make one hundred calls and get thirty people to answer, you might get one or two appointments—and our industry calls that a success!

However, if you make one hundred calls a day to get thirty people on the phone, you will spend a solid three to four hours just doing calls. Do that five days in a row. Then do that another five days the next week. Then keep doing it week after week, month after month.

I haven't seen many, if any, real estate agents disciplined enough to generate leads day after day and truly enjoy cold calling strangers for business. Imagine talking to strangers, and getting a "no" or "not interested" ninety-eight times for every one hundred connections. Those are the typical conversion statistics for the industry. Now imagine doing that every day for the rest of your real estate life, five days a week, fifty weeks a year (assuming you take at least two weeks off for vacation) to get consistent results. That wasn't fun for me, but I did it anyway. It took five and a half hours to dial 200 numbers, get one hundred people on the phone, and end up with two to three appointments. In the early days, before I was confident in my presentation, I would get one, sometimes two, of those people to choose me as their real estate agent.

Generating Leads

There's a myth in real estate that business will fall into your lap. A lot of companies promise to send hundreds of leads directly to real estate agents. Based on my experience and the results I tracked through coaching other top agents, on average, only about 2 percent turn into closed transactions. I study the national averages and compare those statistics with my own results—which is another reason I am writing this book. I feel obligated to let you know that the statistics thrown around the real estate industry are accurate if you consistently, persistently, work a system. Just remember that most statistics and most (if not all) sources for business that you will work or may try will generate a 1 percent, or less, return.

I will share, in the next chapter on "Money," how one study I tracked seemed like an incredible lead generating opportunity. It brought in a lot of money. The reality is, after working that system and tracking it closely, it only got a two times return on investment.

You don't have to settle for the double-up plan. This book is going to share with you how applying the E-Myth principles can capture and convert to get a six- or eight-times return on investment (ROI). These systems can help you capture more business so you do not have to keep your nose to the grindstone looking for the next lead day in and day out for the rest of your career.

Throughout this book, I will reference services and tools you may be paying for now. The takeaway is not necessarily to get rid of everything. In fact, all those services—such as lead capture sites, web enhancements, banner programs, keyword searches, and business tracking spreadsheets—can enhance and help you grow your business, especially when you apply *The E-Myth Real Estate Agent* systems to every one of them. You don't need many of them. What you do need is a business plan for each one you use. You will begin to think like an entrepreneur and manager, holding your dollars accountable for the biggest return possible.

Don't Just Double Your Investment

Do not make snap decisions to buy a product or service. Before you buy anything, determine what your business plan will be to get a five- or ten-times return on that investment. Ask yourself, how fast will I get my return? Don't fall for the deadliest sales pitch of all—that all you need is one sale to get your money back.

I have seen hundreds of agents fall for this. Most will pay into the system for six months to a year to see if they can get that one sale to justify having paid for it. Successful business owners have a strategy to get their return on investment as soon as possible (get into the "black"). Smart business owners have an organized strategy, and know how long it will take to get their investment back and how much of an ROI they want. They probably won't run up too many business investments that just pay their initial investment back. Too many real estate agents just write a check on a good commission month and hope it will pay off.

I have found so many of the top, successful agents in the industry don't manage their money or get a return on investments like a

Fortune 500 company would. Their real estate business is not set up like a franchise with predictable, consistent results.

How many times have you heard someone say, "track your numbers"? So you attended a numbers workshop, or had a coach or mentor give you a detailed spreadsheet of numbers to track. In one of my coaching experiences, I was told to track twenty to thirty different numbers to move to a profitable business. The issue? I was still a technician trying to survive. I was not a manager yet and didn't have time to keep track of all that. I had to go get the next deal to put money in my account.

I have consulted with top agents over the years and realized it wasn't just me: they neither had time nor wanted to track so many different things. When we had a coaching call, we were responsible for bringing our numbers to the call. How many times do you think these top agents showed up with all their numbers? Not very often. However, they were running better-than-average real estate businesses and making a lot of money. They were in coaching because they weren't getting the results they wanted, or their income was not consistent or predictable. They were wandering, looking for the answers to be more successful.

This "wandering" is the first step of what Michael calls "having an entrepreneurial seizure." When it comes to numbers, every business should have a profit-and-loss statement (P&L). However, in the "Money" chapter I am going to share one simple strategy that will tell you instantly—whether you are new a new real estate agent or running a big real estate business—how profitable your company is without a detailed P&L. You can know, at a glance, if you are profitable. This is how you can work toward managing your money like a successful business.

This book will allow you to shortcut all my years of trying to "figure it out." I will share a turnkey system to help you get more implemented in the "Planning" chapter of this book, *The E-Myth Real Estate Agent*. This simple plan will help you work "ON" your business versus just being "IN" your business.

Repetition Is Key to Success

My first year or two in real estate I went to every training, seminar, and real estate conference I could. However, in those first years, even though I attended a lot of events and took a lot of notes, I really wasn't implementing the things I wrote down when I got back to the office.

The breakthrough came when I committed to an eight-week course to master the listing process, and I took the same course over and over about a dozen times until it was sizzled into my brain. That was when I realized becoming masterful at something is more about repetition. The more I repeated the same class over and over, the better chance I would implement that information.

Most people go to a class once or read a book once. Look at your two or three favorite books on your bookshelf. Pull them down and read them ten more times. You will be amazed at what happens. Here is what I discovered from my coaching clients: it was after the fourth, sixth and eighth read that they all had profound changes in their businesses around what they were reading in the book. The first two to three times just get you excited and pumped up. The fourth read is when the dots connect, and a vision or plan begins to surface. In fact, some clients got some things implemented by the fourth read. On the sixth and eighth read, entire business plans and action plans showed up to put more of the ideals, philosophies, and systems into action—and see results.

If real estate agents were taught to apply *The E-Myth* principles to our business, we would have a chance for success earlier in our career. In fact, the subtitle of the book is *Why Most Small Businesses Don't Work and What to Do About It*. That book was written for all of us. The real estate business is no different than any other small business. No matter what level of success you have reached today, if you had applied The E-Myth principles from the start, you would be even more successful. This is my gift to you. This book allows me to give you the real estate perspective of The E-Myth principles and the systems that will help you be more successful than you ever imagined.

Accountability and Consistency

One of my biggest accountability lessons came after my divorce. I simply told my kids what needed to happen for me to be successful. I used to tell them all the time, "If Daddy can sell a house this month, we can go to . . . (zoo, Chuck E. Cheese's, the park, etc.)." The reality was the "IF."

This became one of my most successful accountability tools. Kids won't let you forget anything you said when it involves ice cream, pizza, or other fun kid stuff. I would say, "Hey, kids, if Daddy shows you a list of five names every day for the next six months—five names that I put into daddy's computer every day—then we will go to Disneyland (in six months)." BAM! That was the best thing I ever told my girls. Do you think they held me accountable to put new people in my database every day?

And yes, we did go to Disneyland that year.

Have you read *The E-Myth* or *The E-Myth Revisited?* Remember what Michael said: "If your business isn't growing, it is DYING!" I heard that message early on and knew I absolutely had to add new relationships to my database every single day. Fortunately for me, my girls wanted to go to Disney . . . and we all won.

Another successful tactic I learned was targeted postcard mailing. I printed out an entire six months' worth of postcards, and labeled and stamped everything at the start. The results started paying off in month six. Remember when I said I implemented The E-Myth principles? It is about working smart AND getting to the cash the fastest way possible. Well, most of the time the fastest way to consistent cash is six months to a year down the road. I am not telling you something you haven't heard before. Remember Aesop's fable about *The Tortoise and the Hare* that decided to race? Slow and steady (consistent) wins the race.

Be Among the Top 5 Percent

Once back in Kansas City, I also became aware of the success ratios of real estate agents. Out of all the licensed agents in the country, 5 percent of the agents are getting 95 percent of the business and, vice versa, 95 percent are getting 5 percent of the business. You can verify the numbers yourself. The numbers are on the Multiple Listing Service, and the numbers are the same in just about every major city. You will find that about 50 percent of all agents in an office probably close one to two . . . maybe up to four deals a year, and still many of them are at zero sales. About 20 percent of all the licensees are operating as full-time real estate agents.

What I learned from all these numbers was that I needed to hang around the top 5 percent of agents and do what they were doing to be successful. Whenever I attended a conference or training event, I would go meet all the speakers and shake their hand. Of course, I also got their contact information so I could send them a handwritten note to thank them for sharing. I kept in touch with them to make sure I stayed in front them and their information, which would eventually help me get off the real estate roller-coaster-income ride and build a stable, predictable business.

Those first two years after restarting in Kansas City, I went from $1 million in sales to $2 million in sales in one year. I was copying, implementing, and creating systems that mirrored what other successful agents were doing. PLUS, I had read *The E-Myth Revisited* and layered the E-Myth philosophy into my systems. Over the next couple of years, I successfully doubled and quadrupled my business, going from $2 million to $4 million and from $4 million to $8 million.

The biggest difference I can share with you from my success in real estate is that I never stopped. If you start anything, you must commit to it for a minimum of six months and work it hard. Most people, like me in the early days, give up too soon. They might do something one or two days but not twenty days in a row or sixty days in a row. They quit right before the big payout and return.

Life is truly about enjoying life, having life experiences, and loving those around you. It makes everything worthwhile down the road when you can say you lived an awesome life. Yet one more reason I must share this book and the secrets I learned about money and building a successful real estate business that doesn't "run your life."

You will notice that if you follow and implement these turnkey systems the way I describe, you will have predictable results. This book is going to show you a simple way to double, triple, and eventually get as much as five to six times more business than if you don't implement *The E-Myth Real Estate Agent* systems in your business. Believe me when I say you do not want to learn this business the way I did.

But don't expect this plan to cash in overnight. Keep working for that next deal while you are putting this plan into place. The more consistent you are, the faster you will get off the roller-coaster. Speaking of cash, I will share some simple turnkey systems in the next chapter on "Money." These systems and tips can help you get on the path of running a real estate business, not a real estate practice.

Let's move on to the next chapter and find out what Michael has to teach us about *money*. ✤

CHAPTER 3

On the Subject of Money

Michael E. Gerber

If money is your hope for independence, you will never have it. The only real security that a man will have in this world is a reserve of knowledge, experience, and ability.

—Henry Ford

Had Steve and Peggy first considered the subject of money as we will here, their lives could have been radically different.

Money is on the tip of every real estate agent's tongue and on the edge (or at the very center) of every real estate agent's thoughts, intruding on every part of a real estate agent's life.

With money consuming so much energy, why do so few real estate agents handle it well? Why was Steve, like so many real estate agents, willing to entrust his financial affairs to a relative stranger? Why is money scarce for most real estate agents? Why is there less money than expected? And yet the demand for money is always greater than anticipated.

What is it about money that is so elusive, so complicated, so difficult to control? Why is it that every real estate agent I've ever met hates to deal with the subject of money? Why are they almost always too late in facing money problems? And why are they constantly obsessed with the desire for more of it?

Money—you can't live with it, and you can't live without it. But you'd better understand it and get your people to understand it. Because until you do, money problems will eat your company for lunch.

You don't need an accountant or a financial planner to do this. You simply need to prod your people to relate to money very personally. From the office assistant to the operations manager, they all should understand the financial impact of what they do every day in relationship to the profit and loss of the company.

And so you must teach your people to think like owners, not like technicians, managers, or receptionists. You must teach them to operate like personal profit centers, with a sense of how their work fits in with the company as a whole.

You must involve everyone in the company with the topic of money—how it works, where it goes, how much is left, and how much everybody gets at the end of the day. You also must teach them about the four kinds of money created by the company.

The Four Kinds of Money

In the context of owning, operating, developing, and exiting from a real estate business, money can be split into four distinct but highly integrated categories:

- Income
- Profit
- Flow
- Equity

Failure to distinguish how the four kinds of money play out in your business is a surefire recipe for disaster.

Important Note: Do not talk to your accountants or bookkeepers about what follows; it will only confuse all of you. The information comes from the real-life experiences of thousands of small-business owners, real estate agents included, most of whom were hopelessly confused about money when I met them. Once they understood and accepted the following principles, they developed a clarity about money that could only be called enlightened.

The First Kind of Money: Income

Income is the money a company pays its employees and real estate agents for doing their job *in* the company, including the broker/owner. It's what they get paid for going to work every day.

Clearly, if real estate agents didn't do their job, others would have to, and *they* would be paid the money the company currently pays the real estate agents. Income, then, has nothing to do with *ownership*. Income is solely the province of *employeeship*.

That's why to the real estate agent-as-*employee*, income is the most important form money can take. To the real estate agent-as-*owner*, however, it is the least important.

Most important/least important. Do you see the conflict? The conflict between the real estate agent-as-employee and the real estate agent-as-owner?

We'll deal with this conflict later. For now, just know that it is potentially the most paralyzing conflict in a real estate agent's life.

Failing to resolve this conflict will cripple you. Resolving it will set you free.

The Second Kind of Money: Profit

Profit is what's left over after a real estate business has done its job effectively and efficiently. If there is no profit, the business is doing something wrong.

However, just because the real estate business shows a profit does not mean it is necessarily doing all the right things in the right way. Instead, it just means that something was done right during or preceding the period in which the profit was earned.

The important issue here is whether the profit was intentional or accidental. If it happened by accident (which most profit does), don't take credit for it. You'll live to regret your impertinence.

If it happened intentionally, take all the credit you want. You've earned it. Because profit created intentionally, rather than by accident, is replicable—again and again. And your business's ability to repeat its performance is the most critical ability it can have.

As you'll soon see, the value of money is a function of your business's ability to produce it in predictable amounts at an above-average return on investment.

Profit can be understood only in the context of your real estate business's purpose, as opposed to your purpose as a real estate agent. Profit, then, fuels the forward motion of the company that produces it. This is accomplished in four ways:

- Profit is *investment capital* that feeds and supports growth.
- Profit is *bonus capital* that rewards people for exceptional work.
- Profit is *operating capital* that shores up money shortfalls.
- Profit is *return-on-investment capital* that rewards you, the real estate agent-owner, for taking risks.

Without profit, a real estate business cannot subsist, much less grow. Profit is the fuel of progress.

If a company misuses or abuses profit, however, the penalty is much like having no profit at all. Imagine the plight of a real estate agent who has way too much return-on-investment capital and not enough investment capital, bonus capital, and operating capital. Can you see the imbalance this creates?

The Third Kind of Money: Flow

Flow is what money *does* in a real estate business, as opposed to what money is. Whether the business is large or small, money tends to move erratically through it, much like a pinball. One minute it's there; the next minute it's not.

Flow can be even more critical to a business's survival than profit, because a company can produce a profit and still be short of money. Has this ever happened to you? It's called profit on paper rather than in fact.

No matter how large your company, if the money isn't there when it's needed, you're threatened—regardless of how much profit you've made. You can borrow it, of course. But money acquired in dire circumstances is almost always the most expensive kind of money you can get.

Knowing where the money is and where it will be when you need it is a critically important task of both the real estate agent-as-employee and the real estate agent-as-owner.

Rules of Flow

You will learn no more important lesson than the huge impact flow can have on the health and survival of your real estate business, let alone your business or enterprise. The following two rules will help you understand why this is so critical.

1. **The First Rule of Flow states that your income statement is static, while the flow is dynamic.** Your income statement is a snapshot, while the flow is a moving picture. So, while your income statement is an excellent tool for analyzing your company *after* the fact, it's a poor tool for managing it in the heat of the moment.

Your income statement tells you (1) how much money you're spending and where, and (2) how much money you're receiving and from where.

Flow gives you the same information as the income statement, plus it tells you *when* you're spending and receiving money. In other words, flow is an income statement moving through time. And that is the key to understanding flow. It is about management in real time. How much is coming in? How much is going out? You'd like to know this daily, or even by the hour if possible. Never by the week or month.

You must be able to forecast flow. You must have a flow plan that helps you gain a clear vision of the money that's out there next month and the month after that. You must also pinpoint what your needs will be in the future.

Ultimately, however, when it comes to flow, the action is always in the moment. It's about *now*. The minute you start to meander away from the present, you'll miss the boat.

Unfortunately, few real estate agents pay any attention to flow until it dries up completely and slow pay becomes no pay. They are oblivious to this kind of detail until, say, a contract falls through. That gets a real estate agent's attention because the expenses keep on coming.

When it comes to flow, most real estate agents are flying by the proverbial seat of their pants. No matter how many people you hire to take care of your money, until you change the way you think about it, you will always be out of luck. No one can do this for you.

Managing flow takes attention to detail. But when flow is managed, your life takes on an incredible sheen. You're swimming with the current, not against it. You're in charge!

2. **The Second Rule of Flow states that money seldom moves as you expect it to.** But you do have the power to change that, provided you understand the two primary sources of money as it comes in and goes out of your real estate business.

The truth is, the more control you have over the *source* of money, the more control you have over its flow. The sources of money are both inside and outside your company.

Money comes from *outside* your company in the form of receivables, commissions, reimbursements, investments, and loans.

Money comes from *inside* your company in the form of payables, taxes, capital investments, and payroll. These are the costs associated with attracting clients, delivering your services, operations, and so forth.

Few real estate agents see the money going *out* of their company as a source of money, but it is.

When considering how to spend money in your company, you can save—and therefore make—money in three ways:

- Do it more effectively.
- Do it more efficiently.
- Stop doing it altogether.

By identifying the money sources inside and outside your company, and then applying one or more of the alternatives listed above, you will be immeasurably better at controlling the flow in your company.

But what are these sources? They include how you:

- Manage your services
- Buy supplies and equipment
- Compensate your people
- Plan people's use of time
- Determine the direct cost of your services
- Increase the number of clients seen
- Manage your work
- Collect reimbursements and receivables

In fact, every task performed in your agency (and ones you haven't yet learned how to perform) can be done more efficiently and effectively, dramatically reducing the cost of doing business. In the process, you will create more income, produce more profit, and balance the flow.

The Fourth Kind of Money: Equity

Sadly, few real estate agents fully appreciate the value of equity in their real estate business. Yet equity is the second most valuable asset any real estate agent will ever possess. (The most valuable asset is, of course, your life. More on that later.)

Equity is the financial value placed on your real estate business by a prospective buyer.

Thus, your *business* is your most important product, not your services. Because your business has the power to set you free. That's right. Once you sell your business—providing you get what you want for it—you're free!

Of course, to enhance your equity, to increase your business's value, you have to build it right. You have to build an business that works. A company that can become a true business and a business that can become a true enterprise. A company/business/enterprise that can produce income, profit, flow, and equity better than any other real estate agent's company can.

To accomplish that, your business must be designed so it can do what it does systematically and predictably, every single time.

The Story of McDonald's

Let me tell you the most unlikely story anyone has ever told you about the successful building of a real estate company, business, and enterprise. Let me tell you the story of Ray Kroc.

You might be thinking, "What on earth does a hamburger stand have to do with my company? I'm not in the hamburger business; I'm a real estate agent."

Yes, you are. But by practicing real estate as you have been taught, you've abandoned any chance to expand your reach, help more clients, or improve your services the way they must be improved if the business of real estate—and your life—are going to be transformed.

In Ray Kroc's story lies the answer.

Kroc called his first McDonald's restaurant "a little money machine." That's why thousands of franchisees bought it. And the reason it worked? Kroc demanded consistency, so that a hamburger in Philadelphia would be an advertisement for one in Peoria. In fact, no matter where you bought a McDonald's hamburger in the 1950s, the meat patty was guaranteed to weigh exactly 1.6 ounces, with a diameter of 3⅝ inches. It was in the McDonald's Operations Manual.

Did Kroc succeed? You know he did! And so can you, once you understand his methods. Consider just one part of his story.

In 1954, Kroc made his living selling the five-spindle Multi-mixer milkshake machine. He heard about a hamburger stand in San Bernardino, California, that had eight of his machines in operation, meaning it could make forty shakes simultaneously. This he had to see.

Kroc flew from Chicago to Los Angeles, then drove sixty miles to San Bernardino. As he sat in his car outside Mac and Dick McDonald's restaurant, he watched as lunch customers lined up for bags of hamburgers.

In a revealing moment, Kroc approached a strawberry blonde in a yellow convertible. As he later described it, "It was not her sex appeal but the obvious relish with which she devoured the hamburger that made my pulse begin to hammer with excitement."

Passion.

In fact, it was the French fry that truly captured his heart. Before the 1950s, it was almost impossible to buy fries of consistent quality. Kroc changed all that. "The French fry," he once wrote, "would become almost sacrosanct for me, its preparation a ritual to be followed religiously."

Passion and preparation.

The potatoes had to be just so—top-quality Idaho russets, eight ounces apiece, deep-fried to a golden brown, and salted with a shaker that, as Kroc put it, kept going "like a Salvation Army girl's tambourine."

As Kroc soon learned, potatoes too high in water content—even top-quality Idaho russets vary greatly in water content—come out soggy when fried. And so Kroc sent out teams of workers, armed with hydrometers, to make sure all his suppliers were producing potatoes in the optimal solids range of 20 percent to 23 percent.

Preparation and passion. Passion and preparation. Look those words up in the dictionary, and you'll see Kroc's picture. Can you envision your picture there?

Do you understand what Kroc did? Do you see why he was able to sell thousands of franchises? Kroc knew the true value of equity, and, unlike Steve from our story, Kroc went to work *on* his business rather than *in* his business. He knew the hamburger wasn't his product—McDonald's was!

So what does *your* real estate business need to do to become a little money machine? What is the passion that will drive you to build a company that works—a turnkey system like Ray Kroc's?

Equity and the Turnkey System

What's a turnkey system? And why is it so valuable to you? To better understand it, let's look at another example of a turnkey system that worked to perfection: the recordings of Frank Sinatra.

Frank Sinatra's records were to him as McDonald's restaurants were to Ray Kroc. They were part of a turnkey system that allowed Sinatra to sing to millions of people without having to be there himself.

Sinatra's recordings were a dependable turnkey system that worked predictably, systematically, automatically, and effortlessly to produce the same results every single time—no matter where they were played, and no matter who was listening.

Regardless of where Frank Sinatra was, his records just kept on producing income, profit, flow, and equity, over and over . . . and still do! Sinatra needed only to produce the prototype recording, and the system did the rest.

Kroc's McDonald's is another prototypical turnkey solution, addressing everything McDonald's needs to do in a basic, systematic way so that anyone properly trained by McDonald's can successfully reproduce the results.

And this is where you'll realize your equity opportunity: in the way your company does business, in the way your company systematically does what you intend it to do, and in the development of your turnkey system—a system that works even in the hands of ordinary people (and real estate agents less experienced than you) to produce extraordinary results.

Remember:

- If you want to build vast equity in your company, then go to work *on* your company, building it into a business that works every single time.

- Go to work *on* your company to build a totally integrated turnkey system that delivers exactly what you promised every single time.

- Go to work *on* your company to package it and make it stand out from the real estate businesses you see everywhere else.

Here is the most important idea you will ever hear about your business and what it can potentially provide for you:

The value of your equity is directly proportional to how well your company works. And how well your company works is directly proportional to the effectiveness of the systems you have put into place upon which the operation of your company depends.

Whether money takes the form of income, profit, flow, or equity, the amount of it—and how much of it stays with you—invariably boils down to this. Money, happiness, life—it all depends on how well your company works. Not on your people, not on you, but on the system.

Your business holds the secret to more money. Are you ready to learn how to find it?

Earlier in this chapter, I alerted you to the inevitable conflict between the real estate agent-as-employee and the real estate agent-as-owner. It's a battle between the part of you working in the business and the part of you working on the business. Between the part of you working for income and the part of you working for equity.

Here's how to resolve this conflict:

- Be honest with yourself about whether you're filling *employee* shoes or *owner* shoes.

- As your company's key employee, determine the most effective way to do the job you're doing, *and then document that job.*

- Once you've documented the job, create a strategy for replacing yourself with someone else (another real estate agent) who will then use your documented system exactly as you do.

- Have your new employees manage the newly delegated system. Improve the system by quantifying its effectiveness over time.

- Repeat this process throughout your company wherever you catch yourself acting as employee rather than owner.

- Learn to distinguish between ownership work and employee-ship work every step of the way.

Master these methods, understand the difference between the four kinds of money, develop an interest in how money works in your company . . . and then watch it flow in with the speed and efficiency of a perfectly pounded hammer.

Now let's take another step in our strategic thinking process. Let's look at the subject of *planning*. But first, let's see what Brad has to say about *money*. ❧

CHAPTER 4

Getting a 5- to 10-Times Return on Everything You Do

Brad Korn

A true business opportunity is the one that an entrepreneur invents to grow him or herself. Not to work in, but to work on.
                                             —Michael E. Gerber

When I signed up for my first real estate license class, I thought real estate school would teach me everything I needed to know. The reality is most schools don't cover the topic of money and how to run a profitable business by holding your dollars accountable. My upfront, out-of-pocket expense when I decided to become a real estate agent was the school. To get your mind set for the reading of this chapter, take yourself out of the E-Myth Technician role and put yourself in your Manager role. I would ask, "What is your return on investment for attending real estate license class?" Do you have a business plan to recoup your investment?

Most schools run anywhere from $200 to $400. Unfortunately, most people do not realize how much more will be needed to become a real estate agent. I mentioned in the last chapter that I started out in a deep financial hole. I was looking for my lottery ticket to bail me out. Like many people who get into real estate, this venture may be their last big chance to get out of whatever tough financial situation they are in. They really need this thing to work.

I had barely scraped up what at that time was my $350 fee to get through school. When I was done taking the classes, I learned I needed more money before I could sell a house. I didn't have the additional $1,000 to $1,500 to get access to properties, access to the MLS, and join all the associations I needed to join. And that total doesn't include real estate signs, advertising, letterhead, envelopes, and everything else it takes to run a business. Added to that, most real estate companies take a portion of commissions as well. Some can be up to 50 percent or more in company-split programs; however, the higher the split, the more value and extras they should offer the agents.

Track Your Return on Investment

The real question before you get started is to ask yourself, "Am I thinking like a manager?" Are you thinking about return on investment on every dollar you are going to spend?

I hope this book will help you think differently from now on. What about the company or team you choose to align with? Or, alternatively, what is your return on investment for starting your own brokerage or team? Before you make any of those decisions, think about holding your money accountable. When a company gives you a bunch of stuff for free, yet takes a portion of your commissions, realize that YOU are paying for all that free stuff. The real estate brokerage is a business as well. It must make a profit to keep the doors open so you can have a business.

Nothing is really "free." What I found in all split structures in the real estate industry is that even though you are getting something, like a free office (or cubicle), free copies, an advertising budget, etc., your first sale or two (depending on your average price point) may cost you thousands of dollars for all that "free" stuff.

What I am suggesting is to ask yourself if you are making a return on investment on all those things you might be calling "perks."

Now I am not saying these split structures are bad. However, you need to look at them through your new CEO Manager eyes; look at them from a money perspective. Ask yourself, what is the return on investment (the split you pay the company)? How much more money will you make and how much time will you save with the services they provide?

One thing to be aware of is the plethora of companies that want to sell you their products or services. Be extra cautious. You need to really put on your CEO Money eyes for all the sales calls coming your way. You need to evaluate all the services, tools, and systems that will bombard your phone, your mailbox, and just about every conference you might attend. If you don't carefully evaluate your ROI on every one, you will literally get nickeled and dimed by purchasing $10, $15, $20, and $30 real estate-related things that promise to blow up your business.

I'm not suggesting you shouldn't use any of these services and tools in your business, I am simply sharing that I wish I had known early in my real estate career that I was not thinking like a manager. I needed to think about what my business plan was going to be to get a five- to ten-times return on every one of those items. Here is a script you can use on your next solicited phone call that will move you toward that CEO mind-set. Maybe this script can save you thousands of dollars each year the way it did for me—by not signing up for something I wouldn't have used or that wouldn't have worked.

The next time the phone rings, and the salesperson starts his pitch, don't hang up! What if this product or service really ends up giving you a five- or ten-times return? Use the following script: "Your product sounds great. Can you guarantee me a five- to ten-times return on my investment"?

The salesperson on the phone will not know how to answer this. I just ask them to show me the strategy to get five times the cost of the product or service. If they take the time to do that, and the strategy really could get me that, then I will keep listening.

Most of the time, however, this script will save you five more minutes of your life, and you can get a five- to ten-times bigger return on your time by not listening to another sales pitch.

Plan for a 10-Times ROI

Think about it. If you planned to get ten times more results before you purchased your next "real estate success item" and it cost $30 per month, a ten-times return would make you $300 per month, or $3,600 for the entire year. The salespeople for small-ticket items have a script most agents will fall for. They say, "All you need is ONE sale, and it will pay for itself." The reality is it could take several months to get that one sale, or you might only get one sale the entire time you are using that product or service. If you put that in place and you had your first sale from that item in just thirty days, you would have gotten a ten-times return on your investment. Most agents don't track it, and as I mentioned in the last chapter, I would try something for a few weeks or few months, and then give it up because it didn't work. Guess what? Most providers of that item won't call you in three months to see how it is going or ask if you have made a ten-times return. They will, however, continue to charge your card every month even if you haven't recouped your initial investment. Some of those amounts are so small you may not even realize you are spending money.

In my early days of real estate, I wasn't tracking anything except the balance in my checking account. One time I went to a seminar where they talked about getting a return on investment. The idea I got was to cancel all my credit cards and get new numbers. That one tip saved me about $200 to $300 per month because I had signed up for a dozen little $10- to $30-per-month items. I mentioned earlier how bad this real estate gig needed to work. I was desperate to be successful and support my family, yet in just a couple of years I was losing all that money every month and doing nothing with the stuff I was paying for.

Please don't make the same mistake. Don't cancel your cards to cancel all that stuff. I am going to share the models or systems to turn anything you currently pay for into real money and get a five- to ten-times return. If you are paying for something that is not getting you a return right now, this book will give you a plan to get rid of expenses that are costing you money, rather than making you money. Simply apply the systems I talk about throughout the book, and you will begin to get a return on investment for everything you do.

The trap I fell into was the common assumption, "You have to spend money to make money."

Find the Fastest Way to Profits

WRONG! If you are going to spend money to make money, then make sure you find the fastest way to the cash (profit). How much money will be generated because of the money you are spending? It is OK to hold a company accountable to you for getting a return on investment when you use its product or service. It is OK to hold a business coach accountable for getting you a five- to ten-times return when you hire him or her to help you with your business. I have gotten a little extreme over the years because I even hold my letterhead and envelopes accountable for getting me a return on investment.

My margin of profit selling real estate in the Midwest is not as large as someone in San Diego or New York. However, just because you may be in a market where your average commission is more than some people make in an entire year doesn't mean you should be frivolous with your money. You can keep the same standards I mention throughout this book and get crazy profit margins. Imagine what a five- to ten-times return on investment would be if you received a $10,000 commission check and spent it on something that truly gave you that high a return on investment. You would leverage an additional $100,000 from that $10,000. No matter how you look at it, that is more money than you would have had before you read this book. A lot more! I personally know a LOT of agents who spend

$2,000 to $20,000 or more each month to run their business, and they are not bringing in $200,000 per month. All the money being wasted in the real estate industry is putting agents out of business.

The industry is full of companies that promise huge results with very little effort on your part. In fact, "lead generation" is probably one of the most overused phrases in our industry. Most, if not all, agents I have met throughout my career really do not like lead generating. I know because in all my years of observing thousands of agents, I noticed that picking up the phone and calling a new lead is one of the first things agents want to give away or hire to be done, or they just return calls when it is convenient for them. They want someone else to do all the lead generation, so they can do what they really like to do, which typically isn't picking up the phone for two to four hours every day to convert another lead.

It is hard to see how you would lose money and get yourself on a path to go out of business when you are paying just $30 per month for a website that promises hundreds—if not thousands—of leads. There are now companies charging $1,500 to $3,000 (or more) per month to generate thousands of leads.

Track Your Conversion Rates

Let me share one system to get a handle on "tracking your dollars." This one system will change the way you think about the money being spent in your real estate business. Track your leads, how many dials you make, how many people answer the phone, how many will meet you, and finally, how many of them close and put commission dollars in your bank account. Once you know your conversion rates, you can determine what your ROI is for that lead source and determine if it is worth the risk to write the check every month.

You probably heard me mention how I have built my business on relationships and kept in touch with those people on a more consistent, persistent basis than most other real estate agents. People have been researching and tracking conversion rates of internet leads for years. In fact, I took part in one research study where a group of top agents tracked the true conversion rate for internet leads. The result was, at best, about a 2 percent to 3 percent conversion rate. I have taken the results from that study and created a strategy to get five times more conversion over time.

Leverage What You Spend

I have not had to rely on "buying leads" because my database runs efficiently, and my phone rings on a consistent basis with new business opportunities. However, while I was studying other agents and the industry, I noticed many of them signed up for high-dollar lead generation sites. The results from these sites were positive, and it was hard to lose money on some of them, especially when they were designed to have other vendors and affiliates help defer the cost while staying in compliance with industry rules and laws. I decided to sign up for one of them to track the results.

The cost was approximately $2,400 per month. Over the first year I invested $28,800. We closed 24 sales directly related to this service. Our average commission check was $4,000, so that was $92,000 in commission gained. Now, take the splits into account. These were pretty much all buyers, and I had a buyer's agent working with all those buyers. If we split the commission, that would have been $46,000 to my agent and $46,000 to the team. The team was "on the hook" for the $28,800 paid in, so by the time you take that out of the $46,000 in income, that left a profit of $17,200. Keep in mind this is not taking into consideration the real estate broker or company split.

Our buyer's agent LOVED this new system. The agent had no expense AND earned $46,000 in profit from this one system. For me, the business owner, this was nowhere near a five-times or ten-times return on investment. In fact, I was on the hook for $28,800 every year, even if we didn't close a deal. Being a business owner who was following the E-Myth principles, I was holding my money accountable. I wanted to see at least $144,000 in profit every year after our team split and expenses.

Most agents would say, "Hey, I didn't lose money; in fact, I made $17,000." That is a lot of money and not a losing proposition. However, as I will share with you in this book, there are higher-leveraged things you could do with the same $28,800 or $2,400 per month. There are opportunities that can make you $288,000 in profit or more!

We captured 1,000 leads our first year using that system. We had good, two-way conversations with one hundred of those leads, whom we added into our database. Twenty-four of them closed and sold. That is what I call the "fall-out-of-the-sky, easy business" anyone should be able to get. The big loss is when an agent thinks that is a great deal, and they don't think about the lost opportunity from a five-times to ten-times return.

I said earlier, I take systems and ideas, and master them to win big. My focus for year two was to get seventy five closed transactions over the next year and 300 leads into our database. That focus on seventy five closed transactions would have generated $150,000 to the team for the year, less the same $28,800 expense and been a profit of $121,200 over the $17,000 profit from the first year. THAT is a GREAT return from the same amount of leads by focusing on better conversion results. Unfortunately, after three years of tracking and tweaking, the team did not get the numbers up that high. We dropped that lead generation site from our budget. I see so many agents stay with a plan like this because they aren't losing money, yet they put so much time and effort into managing the system they are not aware of missed opportunities.

So let's talk about the four kinds of money—Income, Profit, Flow, and Equity—and how these relate to your real estate business. Keep in mind, the business principles we are talking about here are not under-stood by everyone. Don't hand this information to your accountant or bookkeeper and ask them to "track it," unless they have read *The E-Myth Bookkeeper*.

Let's Start With Income

I only get paid when a transaction closes. That was a huge lesson for me to learn.

A lot goes into every transaction to get it closed. You can make a list of at least ninety-nine things that must happen from contract to closing—and that's not even everything. Your income could be limited by the number of transactions you can physically close by yourself. An easy fix would be to hire someone to help. In fact, in some real estate markets the commission check at closing is a huge dollar amount! But that doesn't mean you should run right out and hire someone to help because you made one large commission.

Those big checks can be an agent's downfall. Big checks make them think they can invest (or spend) more money on their business. Someone who makes $10,000 to $20,000 from one sale might jump the gun on adding more people to the team in order to give away the stuff they don't want to do or don't really like to do, like cold calling for business. If the money being spent doesn't bring a return, that agent will have increased expenses more than the business's income—and won't realize it until it is too late. The danger is committing to monthly expenses during the busy months, then finding out they are still on the real estate income roller coaster, and the money dries up one month. Now that agent has a huge monthly money commitment without sustained growth. That real estate agent didn't hold those new commitments accountable for a return on investment.

I was fortunate to start my real estate career in the Midwest because our average price point is so much lower than in many other parts of the country. I was forced to make every minute count to get as many closings as possible and to hold every dollar accountable to bring me more dollars. Today I still think in terms of, "Can we close three times more transactions with the current system and not cause everyone to quit or burn out?" Like the previous example, the return on investment from $17,000 to $120,000 was just closing more deals with the same amount of leads. You must close more to make more. Just spending more to make more won't necessarily increase your profit.

It's Much More Fun to Talk About Profit

I didn't track profit in the early days of my real estate career because I didn't understand the manager part of my business. It is truly an industry-wide issue because real estate agents are not taught the basic principles of running a business. When my commission checks came in for me, I just put them in my checking account and kept rolling. I was dumping money in as fast as I made it—and spending it just as fast. If I could pay all my bills and had even one dollar left over, I considered mine a profitable business. There were months when I couldn't pay bills because I was spending money faster than it was coming in. The trouble occurred when my offer on a big property was accepted, and the commission check was going to be double what I usually got. I would go buy something fun or spend the money before the property closed. Here is a simple business lesson: if you spend more than you put in your bank account, you do not have a profitable business.

How Does Your Money Flow?

Sure, I had heard about income statements, and profit and loss statements. Many Fortune 500 CEOs review P&Ls daily, and they would never make business decisions without them. But if I gave you a spreadsheet today to track every dollar and the percentages you need to spend in certain areas, your eyes would gloss over. Many times, we are given too much to track when our focus is staying alive, paying our monthly bills, and getting the next deal.

In the beginning, I tried a strategy of putting an entire month of commission checks in my desk drawer. I thought if I didn't put them in the checking account, I wouldn't spend the money. I did manage to get a full month's worth of commission checks in my desk drawer. That was the first time I felt like I was getting my money situation under control. The comfort for me was knowing I would be one month ahead of my expenses and not have to stress about paying my bills. It was great that first month.

However, I eventually found myself back on that income roller-coaster because I fell behind and had to deposit those checks early.

You may be like me and hate tracking numbers, or maybe you don't consider yourself busy enough to track all that. Let me share with you the simplest way to get your money under control and track your profit so you can start moving toward that business owner role. Even if you currently track a detailed P&L statement, I have a simple strategy that will make the P&L work the way you intend it to work.

If you want an easy way to see how your money flows from your real estate business to your personal life, I suggest you implement the following system. In fact, even when you get your money under control and begin tracking your money with income statements and P&L statements, you will want to keep this simple strategy in place. It's setting up a capital account for your business and a separate spending account for your business. That way you will know at a glance if you are profitable without having to review a detailed P&L. Use that to determine your ROI or find out where you are out of budget.

Don't stop there, though. My strategy is to set up four bank accounts. Two accounts will be used for business, and two will be personal accounts. Account number one is your *real estate capital account*. The next is your business *checking account*. The third is your *personal capital account*, and the last one is your *personal checking account*.

Account Summary

Business Checking, Savings and Money Market Accounts

		Account Number	Current Balance*		Available Balance
Rewards Money Market	Capital	_____ XXXXX	$20,549.23	*All Commissions Deposited Here*	$20,549.23
Commercial Checking	Operating	_____ XXXXX	$3,073.78	*Only what is needed for Expenses this week or month*	$2,821.81
			$23,623.01		$23,371.04

1) Business Capital Account: Every commission dollar you earn goes into this account. You will pull out of this account what you need to run your business. However, you will only pull what you need to cover your expenses and you only want to do this once or twice each month.

2) Business Checking Account: You need to know exactly what it costs to run your real estate business every month. Once you have figured that out, you only put that amount in this account each month. Leave any extra commission dollars in your business capital account. If you run short in your checking account, take a moment to figure out why. Did you forget some expenses? Perhaps you have a few flexible expenses. Get your monthly amount as accurate as possible. You will also transfer money from your business capital account into this account to fund your personal account. Then you will write a check from this business account to your personal capital account.

3) Personal Capital Account: This is where you put all the money you pay yourself out of your business to live on. This account may also include your savings, or X dollars you put aside each month to fund a big purchase.

4) Personal Checking Account: This is your personal spending money. How much does it cost to fund your life every month? Pay the bills every month? Etc. Only put in your personal checking account what you spend for that entire month. If by chance you find your personal checking account out of money on the twentieth of the month, you are out of budget. Be careful: don't just put more money into the account without recalculating.

A huge step in implementing *The E-Myth Real Estate Agent* principles into your business is to understand why your business isn't profitable. When your accounts run short, understand why. Find out where the differences are. As Michael explained in the previous chapter, money very seldom flows as you expect it to. When an account is out of money, figure out why and correct it, so it doesn't happen again.

I purposely have set up the capital accounts at my bank as mutual fund accounts that only allow a limited amount of withdrawals each month, or I get charged. Also, if they charge you for being under a certain balance, that is good. It forces you to get that balance in there and keep it there.

When you first start this plan, you will find that you put everything in your business capital account and take everything right back out. That is because you do not have profit this month. There is a two- to three-month delay in the real estate industry from the time you get a new client to the time you get a commission check. So be prepared to stay diligent and watch the flow of your money.

You may find out you haven't ever had any profit. This is one of the first steps to getting off the roller-coaster-income ride. On the personal side, you can take money from your personal capital account and put it in a true savings account. You could do without the personal capital account if you write checks to your savings account as soon as you deposit your personal check from your business checking account. Once you stick to this persistently and consistently, you will see your capital account build up. This is how I finally got a three-month supply of expenses in the bank. Operating everything out of one account is not how CEOs of Fortune 500 companies run their businesses. Real businesses have capital accounts and spending accounts. Start running your real estate "practice" like a true business. You can implement this strategy today! In fact, set this book down now, go to your bank, and set up those accounts. You will be glad you did.

Does Your Current Money Strategy Work?

If you have heard of the "team" concept in real estate, you will find that a variety of formulas and structures exist. No one has figured out "one perfect split structure." Do you want to know if your current money system is enough to live on? Or if you would be able to support adding people to your business at some point in the future? The first step is to separate you from the business. What I mean by that is that you live off the split structure you expect your team to live off of even before you create the team. Are you able to live the lifestyle you want under the terms you would expect anyone else to live if they came to work for you?

I implemented and tweaked *The E-Myth Real Estate Agent* systems for fifteen years prior to opening a second real estate team in another city. We structured the team from the beginning as if we were already a large team. The rainmaker, the main agent, started out as a single agent. We set up our capital and business checking accounts. Anytime the agent worked with a buyer, he paid his personal account the amount of commission we would have paid a buyer's agent. Any time he listed a house, he paid himself the amount we would pay a listing specialist. Keep in mind there are a lot more expenses involved with the listing side of a real estate business. Therefore the commission split is much less than the buyer's agent split.

I found that real estate agents who are not tracking their dollars will most likely spend 60 percent to 70 percent of the total commission dollars earned to run a real estate business. The most efficient team I have ever heard of in my entire career was operating at a 35 percent net profit. Keep that in mind before you start building a team and throw out high commission splits just because another agent said he or she does it that way. First, run your one agent more profitably before you add expenses. Agents are not taught to track their return on investment. As *The E-Myth* suggests, they are technicians who don't run their business like a Fortune 500 company.

Learn from my mistakes. I didn't track my return on investment in my first ten-plus years, and we almost went out of business several times. I took out $20,000 loans every couple of years to keep the real estate business going. I always paid those loans back. But a business model that requires loans to stay in operation is not a good business model. It is stressful to borrow money to stay in real estate. If my business were profitable, I wouldn't have to take out loans or get commission advances from high-fee companies to get survival money. Your business should be able to support itself and have a profit each month. There will be a lot less stress in your life, and in your family life, if you know you are profitable every month.

Do you know how much money you spend to do everything you do? I calculated what it cost me to take a listing. I had run my business long enough to know exactly what marketing activities helped our properties sell faster and for more money. When I calculated the actual out-of-pocket dollars to take a listing, I was shocked to find out I was spending $800 of my personal money the day a seller signed on the listing agreement—and I wouldn't get any money until the deal closed. The cost of the flyers, our monthly advertising in print and on websites, etc. meant we were investing $800 in a listing before we even put a sign in the yard.

I will ask again: do you know what you are spending? It really doesn't cost that much to put a sign in the yard and a property on the internet. In a hot market, that may be all you think you need to do. However, if you had a marketing strategy and spent your money for five times the return on that marketing plan, you would bring more value to your clients and maybe make them more equity from their property than you would without a strategy.

I learned that most of the free or low-cost marketing tactics agents do for sellers, such as flyer boxes and signs in the yard, are all things sellers can do themselves. Those marketing methods did not get crazy, awesome results. A sign in the yard might prompt one direct call to your office for every fifty to one hundred people who drive by. A system that gives the potential buyer information about the home and captures their contact information immediately will get you a better return on your lead-capture system. If you are not tracking your marketing for a return, you are leaving a lot of commission dollars unclaimed. I tracked my marketing to ensure we were getting a return on the investment of taking that listing. My goal is to get three buyers off every listing, even if the listing sold the same day we listed. We kept working until we figured out what got us the best return.

Once you understand what money is coming in, how much profit you have, and where your money is going, you can figure out how to do more in less time, with less money and fewer people (That is, make your people more efficient). Implementing systems will carry the weight and leverage before you hire another person to handle them. Hiring people costs you. It takes away from your profit before they produce more dollars for the bottom line. You start paying salary and hourly fees the day they start, and you won't know ahead of time if they will provide a five- to ten-times higher return on their salary.

We have streamlined our business to be more efficient and effective in every transaction, so we can do three times more business in less time and, most importantly, not sacrifice the client experience. In the Planning chapter of this book, I am going to give you the biggest success secret to running your business more efficiently and how you can automate 80 percent of your business. The best part is the team buy-in you will get. The most important part is the accountability for each person involved in your business. Even if you are an individual agent, you rely on a lot of people to make sure that commission check happens. If you have been in real estate for a while, you already know you can't rely on everyone to do their job well. These turnkey systems will help you get that control back, so you can have a predictable business.

Do You Have Equity in Your Business?

Would someone buy your real estate business? How much would you sell your business for? If you have a price, would you write a check for that amount now and buy your business for that price? If you are not interested in building a big real estate team or life is good if you sell ten to twenty homes a year, congratulations. However, don't pat yourself on the back yet.

I will ask again, what is the equity in your business right now? What if you didn't come in tomorrow, or the next day, or the next? What if something tragic happened to you or a family member, and you had to take off for two weeks? What if you had to be gone for more than five months like I did? I was out of my business for five solid months during Sonya's coma, and several more months before and after that.

We only had two people on the team, and my real estate business closed ninety seven transactions that year.

The reality is, you have the opportunity now to create a business that runs whether you are there or not. That is why I am writing this book! I want to share with you how to turn your real estate opportunity into a business you love and that your family will love. When you create a business that runs whether you are there or not, and your business grows every year, you can focus on what you want to focus on and get more from your life.

Most real estate agents end up selling real estate until they die, or they just quit and walk away from it all. When you build a business with a team of people, and you are able to give them a great lifestyle for their families, then you have a business that can be sold.

So where do you start? When you look at a business with a system that produces predictable results—one that is the same no matter where you go, like McDonalds or Starbucks—then you have found a business worth modeling. There is a very specific path to follow, and it begins by implementing Step 1, then Step 2, etc.

Implementation That Works

The best process to get you started implementing is to put all those ideas running through your head on paper. What helped me start implementing consistently and persistently was to get my top five or ten best ideas on paper. Once I pull those ideas out of my mess of notes, I narrow that list down to my top three ideas. Those top three ideas have a due date and a list of people to help me implement them. Once I get my thoughts organized, I go to work on the first idea.

Start systematizing everything you do. Real estate does not have to be an unpredictable business. In fact, it is not. A typical agent may decide to do an open house on Sunday morning, show up that day and put up a sign up that says Open House. However, if you want a successful open house, wouldn't it be worthwhile to take a little extra time to create a strategy that ensures you have a large number of people come to your open house? Make everything you do count! I created my "Ultimate Open House" system to ensure the best results possible. If I am going to be away from my family for half a day on a weekend, I am going to make sure it is worthwhile and get the most people possible through that front door. I need more sales if I am going to provide the best life possible for my family. I don't spend several hours away from my family on the weekend just to see if I might get more business.

Develop a World-Class Experience for Clients

So where do you start with the turnkey systems?

There are three key areas to focus on for increased business and income for your business. It is the three-legged stool:

1. Get more leads
2. Convert those leads
3. Develop a client fulfillment system (which I refer to as the client experience)

The average person moves every five to seven years, according to past National Association of Realtors® statistics. I personally built my systems to ensure that someone who is going to make one of the biggest financial purchases of their lives—something they do only once every seven years or so—will enjoy the process. Shouldn't it be the same experience a six-year-old has when he or she goes to Disneyland?

I created our systems to deliver a world-class experience for our clients, so they will want to buy another house. I don't want them to have an experience where they say, "We are never doing this again; we will die here before we move again." That doesn't do much for our future business, and I am certain you will not get many referrals if that is the experience your clients are having.

There are a lot of moving parts in a typical real estate transaction. I always say, "If I have to remember to do something, it most likely will not get done." Real estate transactions can be unpredictable, and all the parts of a transaction are constantly moving or changing. The more I can implement checkpoints at each step, the better chance everything will get done, I will deliver world-class service, and I will get more referrals and repeat business.

If I have to remember to do something, It most likely will not get done.

The secret to the systems I am sharing with you in this book is simple. Maybe too simple. The fact is, anyone can do this. Don't make it more difficult than it is.

Don't try to automate it too much, but automate enough to get the right stuff off your plate, so you can take care of all the curve balls thrown your way.

The most complicated part of the entire process is setting it up. The best part about setting up systems is that, once you do so, you don't have to touch them again except to improve or add things. There may be glitches when you first start running the system. However, once you fix them, they are fixed forever. Think McDonalds. It is the same burger every time. Same fries every time. You can have a real estate business where every transaction is predictable, and you know exactly how long it takes to do everything.

It is possible. I did it.

Start looking at your business as though it were a big, monster real estate team, even if you plan to be one agent for the rest of your career. When you look at your business as if every piece of the real estate transaction is a part of the business, you will begin to make everything more efficient.

Why Do People Love Working With You? Document It!

Write down and document everything that makes YOU so good. That way, when you begin to hire people, your expectations will be defined. Everyone will know how they can reproduce the results you get when you do it yourself.

If you already have people working for you, I am sure you have days where you feel a little frustrated. What is causing most of your frustration is the fact that you have not documented why people love working with you. You have not documented your "standards," and no one you hire will ever understand your standards—what you do naturally and don't even realize you are doing. They are not you, and even if you tell them how you do it, they are going to miss something you expect and your clients expect. If you have not documented your own systems in detail, I can assure you there will be things you do naturally that will slip through the cracks, and it may be the one thing that makes your clients love working with you.

Involve everyone who has anything to do with your business in the planning process. Once you learn how to create the perfect process and document it, you will be able to invite others to join you in that process. This will be a revolutionary change in your business; it will lift the weight off your shoulders. You won't have to carry the entire weight of the business. The perfect process I share with you will get complete team buy-in, and their participation in the process will make your clients' experience even better.

When you work through this process you will have the blueprint to automate your entire business, whether you come in every day or can't be there for a month or a year. When you systematize YOU, your business will continue to run and grow even if you're gone. These strategies and systems will turn your job and your role into a business that delivers the level of service you expect for your clients, and your business will grow even without you there.

Buckle up! This next chapter on planning is about to change your entire future in real estate. When you get this, and you implement these processes, the vision of where you and your real estate business are going will get bigger than you ever imagined.

This is the perfect place to see what Michael has to say about *planning*. ❧

CHAPTER 5

On the Subject of Planning

Michael E. Gerber

People in an organization operating from a creative mode . . . approach planning first by determining what they truly want to create, thus in essence becoming true to themselves.
—Robert Fritz, *The Path of Least Resistance*

Another obvious oversight revealed in Steve and Peggy's story was the absence of true planning.

Every real estate agent starting his or her own business must have a plan. You should never begin to see clients without a plan in place. But, like Steve, most real estate agents do exactly that.

A real estate agent lacking a vision is simply someone who goes to work every day. Someone who is just doing it, doing it, doing it. Busy, busy, busy. Maybe making money, maybe not. Maybe getting something out of life, maybe not. Taking chances without really taking control.

The plan tells anyone who needs to know *how we do things here*. The plan defines the objective and the process by which you will attain it. The plan encourages you to organize tasks into functions, and then helps people grasp the logic of each of those functions. This in turn permits you to bring new employees up to speed quickly.

There are numerous books and seminars on the subject of business management, but they focus on making you a better real estate agent. I want to teach you something you've never been taught before: how to be a manager. It has nothing to do with conventional company management and everything to do with thinking like an entrepreneur.

The Planning Triangle

As we discussed in the Preface, every real estate agent sole proprietorship is a company, every real estate business is a company, and every real estate enterprise is a company. Yet the difference between the three is extraordinary. Although all three may offer real estate services, how they do what they do is completely different.

The trouble with most companies owned by real estate agents is that they are dependent on the real estate agent. That's because they're a sole proprietorship—the smallest, most limited form a company can take. Sole proprietorships are formed around the technician, whether real estate agent or heating technician.

You may choose in the beginning to form a company, but you should understand its limitations. The company called a *sole proprietorship* depends on the owner—that is, the real estate agent. The company called a *business* depends on other people plus a system by which that business does what it does. Once your company becomes a business, you can replicate it, turning it into an *enterprise*.

Consider the example of Sea Real Estate. The clients don't come in asking for Douglas Sea, although he is one of the top real estate agents around. After all, he can only handle so many clients a day and be in only one location at a time.

Yet he wants to offer his high-quality services to more people in the community. If he has reliable systems in place—systems any qualified team member can learn to use—he has created a business, and it can be replicated. Douglas can then go on to offer his services—which demand his guidance, not his presence—in a multitude of different settings. He can open dozens of real estate agencies, none of which needs Douglas Sea himself, except in the role of entrepreneur.

Is your real estate business going to be a sole proprietorship, a business, or an enterprise? Planning is crucial to answering this all-important question. Whatever you choose to do must be communicated by your plan, which is really three interrelated plans in one. We call it the Planning Triangle, and it looks like this:

- The Business Plan
- The Deal Plan
- The Completion Plan

The three plans form a triangle, with the business plan at the base, the deal plan in the center, and the completion plan at the apex.

The
Completion
Plan

The Deal Plan

The Business Plan

The Business Plan determines *who* you are (the business). The Practice Plan determines *what* you do (the specific focus of your company). The Completion Plan determines *how* you do it (Client Fulfillment Process and Client Acquisition Process).

By looking at the Planning Triangle, we see that the three critical plans are interconnected. The connection between them is established by asking the following questions:

1. *Who are we?* Purely a strategic question

2. *What do we do?* Both a strategic and a tactical question

3. *How do we do it?* Both a strategic and a tactical question

Strategic questions shape the vision and destiny of your business, of which your company is only one essential component. Tactical questions turn that vision into reality. Thus, strategic questions provide the foundation for tactical questions, just as the base provides the foundation for the middle and the apex of your Planning Triangle.

First ask: What do we do, and how do we do it *strategically?*

And then: What do we do, and how do we do it *practically?*

Let's look at how the three plans will help you develop your company.

The Business Plan

Your business plan will determine what you choose to do in your real estate business and the way you choose to do it. Without a business plan, your company can do little more than survive. And even that will take more than a little luck.

Without a business plan, you're treading water in a deep pool with no shore in sight. You're working against the natural flow.

I'm not talking about the traditional business plan taught in business schools. No, this business plan reads like a story—the most important story you will ever tell.

Your business plan must clearly describe:

- The business you are creating
- The purpose it will serve
- The vision it will pursue
- The process through which you will turn that vision into a reality
- The way money will be used to realize your vision

Build your business plan with *business* language. Make sure the plan focuses on matters of interest to your lenders and shareholders, not just your agents. It should rely on demographics and psychographics to tell you who buys and why. It should also include projections for return on investment and return on equity. Use it to detail both the market and the strategy through which you intend to become a leader in that market, not as a real estate agent but as a business enterprise.

The business plan, though absolutely essential, is only one of three critical plans every real estate agent needs to create and implement. Now let's take a look at the The Deal Plan.

The Deal Plan

The Deal Plan includes everything a real estate agent needs to know, have, and do in order to deliver his or her promise to a client on time, every time.

Every task should prompt you to ask three questions:

1. What do I need to know?
2. What do I need to have?
3. What do I need to do?

What Do I Need to Know?

What information do I need to satisfy my promise on time, every time, exactly as promised? To identify what you need to know, you must understand the expectations of others, including your clients, your managers, agents, and other employees. Are you clear on those expectations? Don't make the mistake of assuming you know. Instead, create a need-to-know checklist to make sure you ask all the necessary questions.

A need-to-know checklist might look like this:

- What are the expectations of my clients?
- What are the expectations of my administrators?
- What are the expectations of my team members?
- What are the expectations of my staff?

What Do I Need to *Have?*

This question raises the issue of resources—namely money, people, and time. If you don't have enough money to finance operations, how can you fulfill those expectations without creating cash-flow problems? If you don't have enough trained people, what happens then? And if you don't have enough time to manage your company, what happens when you can't be in two places at once?

Don't assume you can get what you need when you need it. Most often, you can't. And even if you can get what you need at the last minute, you'll pay dearly for it.

What Do I Need to Do?

The focus here is on actions to be started and finished. What do I need to do to fulfill the expectations of this client on time, every time, exactly as promised? For example, what exactly are the steps to perform when dealing with a distressed homebuyer whose offer was rejected?

Your clients fall into distinct categories, and those categories make up your business. The best real estate agencies will invariably focus on fewer and fewer categories as they discover the importance of doing one thing better than anyone else.

Answering the question *What do I need to do?* demands a series of action plans, including:

- The objective to be achieved
- The standards by which you will know the objective has been achieved
- The benchmarks you need to reach in order for the objective to be achieved
- The function/person accountable for the completion of the benchmarks
- The budget for the completion of each benchmark
- The time by which each benchmark must be completed.

Your action plans should become the foundation for The Completion Plan. And the reason you need completion plans is to ensure that everything you do is not only realistic but can also be managed.

The Completion Plan

If The Business Plan gives you results and provides you with standards, The Completion Plan tells you everything you need to know about every benchmark in The Deal Plan—that is, how you're going to fulfill client expectations on time, every time, as promised. In other words, how you're going to arrange a referral for a home inspector, the steps you take to guide a first-time buyer through submitting an offer, and your specific closing process.

The Completion Plan is essentially the operations manual, providing information about the details of doing tactical work. It is a guide to tell the people responsible for doing that work exactly how to do it.

Every completion plan becomes a part of the knowledge base of your business. No completion plan goes to waste. Every completion plan becomes a kind of textbook that explains to new employees or new associates joining your team how your company operates in a way that distinguishes it from all other real estate agencies.

To return to an earlier example, The Completion Plan for making a Big Mac is explicitly described in the *McDonald's Operation Manual*, as is every completion plan needed to run a McDonald's business.

The Completion Plan for a real estate agent might include the step-by-step details of how to successfully land a seller's business— in contrast to how everyone else has learned to do it. Of course, every real estate agent knows the general steps to take to land new business. They've learned to do it the same way everyone else has learned to do it. But if you are going to stand out as unique in the minds of your clients, employees, and others, you must invent your own way of doing even ordinary things. Most of that value-added perception will come from your communication skills, your listening skills, your innovative skills in transforming an ordinary visit into a great, value-added client experience.

Perhaps you'll decide that a mandatory part of finding the best options for your homebuyer includes asking specific questions about how the family functions and the specific needs unique to them, and providing a lookbook of various house styles to determine this buyer's ideal preference. If no other real estate agent took the time to dig that deeply into their family's specific needs, you'll immediately set yourself apart. You must constantly raise the questions: *How do we do it here? How should we do it here?*

The quality of your answers will determine how effectively you distinguish your business from every other real estate business on the planet.

Benchmarks

You can measure the movement of your business—from what it is today to what it will be in the future—using business benchmarks. These are the goals you want your business to achieve during its lifetime.

Your benchmarks should include the following:

- Financial benchmarks
- Emotional benchmarks (the impact your company will have on everyone who comes into contact with it)
- Performance benchmarks
- Client benchmarks (Who are they? Why do they come to you? What does your company give them that no one else does?)
- Employee benchmarks (How do you grow people? How do you find people who want to grow? How do you create a school in your company that will teach your people skills they can't learn anywhere else?)

Your business benchmarks will reflect (1) the position your company will hold in the minds and hearts of your clients, employees, and investors; and (2) how you intend to make that position a reality through the systems you develop.

Your benchmarks will describe how your management team takes shape and what systems you need to develop so your managers, just like McDonald's managers, will be able to produce the results for which they will be held accountable.

Benefits of the Planning Triangle

By implementing the Planning Triangle, you will discover such things as:

- What your company will look, act, and feel like when it's fully evolved
- When that's going to happen
- How much money you will make

These, then, are the primary purposes of the three critical plans: (1) to clarify precisely what needs to be done to get what the real estate agent wants from his or her business and life, and (2) to define the specific steps by which it will happen.

First *this* must happen, then *that* must happen. One, two, three. By monitoring your progress, step-by-step, you can determine whether you're on the right track.

That's what planning is all about. It's about creating a standard—a yardstick—against which you will be able to measure your performance.

Failing to create such a standard is like throwing a straw into a hurricane. Who knows where that straw will land?

Have you taken the leap? Have you accepted that the words *business* and *company* are not synonymous? That a sole proprietorship relies on the real estate agent and a business relies on other people plus a system?

Because most real estate agents are control freaks, 99 percent of today's real estate businesses are sole proprietorships, not true businesses.

The result, as a friend of mine says, is that "real estate agents are spending all day stamping out fires when all around them the forest is ablaze."

Because real estate agents are never taught to think like businesspeople, the real estate professional is forever at war with the businessperson. This is especially evident in large, multilocation agencies, where administrators (businesspeople) often try to control real estate agents (entrepreneurs). They usually end up treating each other as combatants. In fact, the single greatest reason real estate agents become entrepreneurs is to divorce such administrators and to begin to reinvent the real estate enterprise.

That's you.

Now the divorce is over, and a new love affair has begun. You're a real estate agent with a plan!

Who wouldn't want to do business with such a person?

Now let's take the next step in our strategic odyssey. Let's take a closer look at the subject of *management*. But before we do, let's read what Brad has to say about *planning*. ❖

CHAPTER 6

Create YOUR Perfect Client Experience

Brad Korn

Thus, the Entrepreneurial Model does not start with a picture of the business to be created but of the customer for whom the business is to be created.
　　　　—Michael E. Gerber, *The E-Myth Revisited: Why Most Small Businesses Don't Work and What to Do About It*

Michael says the three personalities of the E-Myth business owner are the Entrepreneur, the Manager and the Technician. When you get these three personalities in sync, you will experience Zen in your business. Most real estate agents operate as technicians their entire career. We get our license and just start doing it, working hard to get the next real estate deal. It's not our fault we get stuck there. Our entire industry, seminars, books, etc. typically teach us to get the next deal. There is very little preparation, strategizing and planning between the time a real estate agent passes the test and shows his or her first property.

I have been fortunate to develop the gift of "visioning." I see things as they will be in the future. Once I get a clear image of where I am headed, I get busy transforming my life to match it. The vision is so clear I operate as though I am already there.

The first step, for me, was to mentally step away from the everyday stress of growing and running my real estate practice. I needed to run my business like the CEO of a Fortune 500 company, even though it was just ME in the beginning. The first step was to buckle down and put a plan together by documenting what I was doing and what needed to happen to deliver incredible service for my clients. I created action plans and systems to automate the basic steps of any real estate transaction. Once they were in place, I could daydream and create a vision of what my ultimate real estate business would look like.

Write Down Your Vision

The absolute best exercise I've ever done is called "create your A-plus paper." Write down your vision for the future so well, so clearly, and in so much detail that your high school English teacher would have given you an A-plus on it. That's how I started out, and it's a pretty simple but effective way to get started.

For example, let's pretend for a minute that you and I know each other very well. We saw each other regularly at real estate conferences, we often grabbed a bite to eat together, and we kept in touch. Now let's say we haven't seen each other for five years. One day, out of the blue, we bump into each other and I say "Whoa . . . what's up (your name), how are you doing? Great to hear. So, tell me, how is business? What does your business look like today? How many people are working with you? How many houses are you selling? Do you have teams throughout the country or the world? Where are you living? What are you driving?"

You get the picture. How do you want to answer those questions? Imagine what YOU want your life and business to look like in five years. Paint that picture in your mind, then write it down. Make sure to be as detailed as possible, and write it out as though you are going to get an A-plus on your story.

TAKE ACTION: Put the book down for a moment. Write that story. Grab a blank sheet of paper and write. Describe your future as whatever you want it to be. Make it as awesome as you can visually imagine.

Welcome back. You have just created a vision for where you are headed. You don't have to know how to get there. However, you now have an outline on paper of where you want to go. This is a huge part of applying *The E-Myth Real Estate Agent* to your business, and the first step to designing a life and business you can be proud of.

Set BIG Goals

When you set BIG goals, you will blow through all the smaller checkpoints much faster. If you set low, comfortable goals, the human element slows us down as we start to approach those goals. This was so true for me. When I first got my real estate license, I just wanted to sell ONE house and make $10,000 (Right?). I was so focused on getting a sale, I looked for anyone who was buying and selling right now. In my first three years in real estate, I closed five to six transactions, total. I was starving!

Once I read *The E-Myth Revisited* and started applying all the principles in the book, I reset my goal. I learned who the top-selling agent in Kansas City was at that time. I set that agent's volume as my new goal and focused on that number. I doubled my business every year for the next five years, going from zero sales in my first year back in Kansas City to $1 million in sales my second year, $2 million the third, $4 million the fourth, and $8 million the fifth. I don't really know what happened. All I know is that I was focused on a huge number and was trying to get there as fast as possible.

Did you "take action"? If so, you've got your A-plus paper and your big goal in mind. Now ask yourself, what is the NEXT thing

I can do to move me closer to that goal and that future? Can I do anything to make some of the next steps easier, or even unnecessary? For example, one of the most important steps for me in the beginning was to get more leads. I knew that would move me closer to my vision. Once I got more leads, I could focus on converting more of those leads.

Now that you are beginning to connect with your inner Entrepreneur by creating a vision of your new, well-defined future, it's time to bring our Manager into the process to make it happen. The manager is the person who makes things happen and holds everyone accountable for what they are supposed to do. Right now, that "everyone" is you.

Create a Bulletproof, Automated System

As Michael says in *The E-Myth Revisited*, "Talent is over-rated." I learned that during my years managing people in the retail clothing industry, where there is a lot of turnover. So when I was setting up my systems, I realized I had to be the one to create a client fulfillment system that delivered my world-class service (your A-plus paper vision). Once I'd created and used that system, I could give it to ordinary people who would deliver my level of service.

The real estate industry gets a bad rap for consumers having horrible experiences. There are plenty of stories about delayed closings, clients having to come up with thousands of dollars more than expected, or clients finding major but undisclosed issues with a property, and much more. Those horrible experiences mostly happen because someone in the transaction wasn't completely truthful, or maybe they were not good at their job. Either way, the rest of the people in the transaction should not suffer because one person didn't do what was expected of them. If I was going to create a world-class experience, there had to be a way to prevent these things from happening—a bulletproof system to ensure the transaction went smoothly for everyone. I wanted to create an experience that was fun for everyone, one that would encourage them to move again in the future.

Michael E. Gerber taught me to set up my business so I didn't have to be there to run it. Most agents believe people only want to do business with them. In the planning stage of my business I documented what people loved about doing business with me. I wrote down what expectations I had for a transaction, such as returning calls quickly, and keeping the client informed and updated throughout the process. I had the best success when I added reminders to check with other people and make sure everything was moving along as planned.

The Manager in me got my systems and processes documented, and from that I created automated action plans around the entire real estate transaction. The automation allowed me to move toward my vision to help hundreds of people have an incredible real estate experience. The more people I could help, the more secure my future would be.

As I implemented the E-Myth principles and automated my lead generation, lead conversion and client fulfillment, my vision grew even bigger! Now I was selling one hundred homes a year, every year, and doing it without working hard. I had agents wanting to learn my systems. That's when my vision became helping one hundred agents each help one hundred families move and have a great experience. Eventually that vision grew into helping 10,000 people. Now, with the writing of this book, I can help thousands of agents help thousands of people have a great experience in real estate and also create a great life for themselves.

Applying the E-Myth principles in our businesses gives us the opportunity to reverse the success (or should I say failure?) ratios for the entire real estate industry. By focusing on lead capture, lead conversion, and client fulfillment systems, we can reverse the 80/20 principle: 80 percent of all real estate agents can succeed and deliver world-class service. In turn, this will create a lasting need to keep the real estate agent involved in the transaction.

For real estate teams and brokerages, this means the agents who come work with you and who follow the E-Myth systems will be more likely to accomplish their big "whys" and enjoy life. By the way, when you help create that, you keep those people forever.

To deliver an incredible experience, we have to keep our clients informed and avoid giving them the status quo answers most agents rely on when things don't go their way. For example, when a home isn't selling, the standard response is, "Your home hasn't sold because it is overpriced." When real estate agents say that repeatedly, clients blame the agent for not doing enough. When that happens, our real estate industry loses credibility and respect.

If you're going to provide that critique to a client, you must show them WHY the house is overpriced and immediately give them a solution. If you can help your clients understand the market conditions, they will leave the transaction feeling knowledgeable and confident that they chose the right agent. That is how you give your clients an extraordinary experience, and they in turn will refer their friends and family to you.

Now Put It All Together

So how would an automated client fulfillment system work? The reality is that every real estate transaction can present new and different challenges from the last one. Especially in the early days of your business. When real estate agents first get into real estate, it can be weeks or months from one sale to the next. How do newer agents complete a contract confidently when they only do it once or twice in their first several months?

It is called a Contract-to-Close System. It is a system any agent, whether they sell one house a month or thirty properties per month, can follow. The system will keep track of all ninety-nine things that must happen. If the agent follows the system, it will keep things from slipping through the cracks. The system keeps everyone, from one agent to a team of people, accountable for every piece of the transaction. The best part is we build in communication with our clients to keep them informed. The biggest complaint from consumers is always lack of communication from their agent.

Creating our turnkey client fulfillment system allowed us to put more energy and focus on delivering a great experience for our clients. Over the years we continued to get better, further streamline our processes, and systematize better ways to communicate with our clients. To this day, we continue to improve our systems to keep ahead of our competitors. Our listing systems are perfected to get our seller clients the most exposure possible, no matter the market conditions. By getting more people through their property than any other agent can, we get them the most equity possible. We get our buyer clients better houses, and they don't lose out as often in competing situations. In twenty-five years of staying true to the E-Myth principles and creating a duplicable system, we have plugged all the holes in the process.

The traditional real estate agent makes the process WAY more complicated than it needs to be. Setting up real estate systems should be so simple a fifth-grader could do it. I developed the "Perfect Process," which helped me create our entire client fulfillment system in a matter of hours.

How to Develop the 'Perfect Process'

It starts with documenting the things you do every day for every transaction. Once you get the transactional items documented, you can create your "Perfect Process." For example, I have a fully automated "New Listing Until Contract" process. Once we list a home we start that process, and everything that needs to happen to get the most exposure and the most money in the shortest time takes effect. Every marketing step is set in motion, and we can't stop any of them.

11/1
- Check email
- Tried to log on to Brad computer for pics
- Talked to Cathy Pollard in regards to Ridgeview offer
- Filled out audit sheet for Ann Ave.
- Submitted contract for Ann to office
- Wrote on board ↑
- Emailed Ann contract to Stacey
- Found & sent Home Warranty to Stacey for 17th
- Check Email
- Create greensheet for 1508 Ashland
- Filled out audit sheet for ↑
- Submitted 1508 Ashland to office
- Emailed contract to Stacey
- Wrote on Board-Ashland
- Called Christy to delete previous green sheet on Forest Avenue
- Emailed Stacey info on Forest
- Called Paychex to figure out how to get Allison set up on payroll
- Updated Craigslist
- Checked email
- Updated 2407 NE 2nd on MLS + sent out email to all agents about bank approved sales price
- Logged onto Korn computer to get pics

This one process will change an agent's business. However, one crucial set of steps must be added for this to be the "PERFECT PROCESS." Remember what the E-Myth principles have taught us about what is important—the client. Your success is directly related to the CONSUMER'S perceived experience and whether they will tell others about their experience. It doesn't matter how good you are at making everything happen behind the scenes to get them to the finish line. A lot happens from the time an offer is accepted until it closes, and it is not always easy. Even though you are working hard, remember, there is a lot of "dead time" for the consumer in that thirty to forty-five days until closing, and they don't know that you are working on it every day.

In all the back-end systems I have looked at, communication with the client is not built into the process. They need to feel like they always know what is happening and recognize how hard you are working to make this transaction as smooth as possible. They want to know you have everything under control—and most agents don't communicate that enough.

A typical client interaction is mostly what the agent thinks is needed or when a frustrated client calls, upset because he or she hasn't heard that everything is moving forward. It doesn't matter how well you cross your "t's" and dot your "i's," or whether you get the property closed on time. If the consumer feels out of the loop, your customer-experience system just failed. All you have to do to create the perfect customer experience is ask your clients, "What do you expect?" Find out what would blow their socks off. As you create your perfect system, you will hold the entire business and everyone working in your business accountable for their piece of the experience, even if it is just you for now.

I used action plans and campaigns to create our systems—everything from lead follow-up to the client fulfillment system and even the lead generation side of the business. Action plans are a series of events that happen once the process is started. I looked at our business plan to deliver an incredible experience and set the standards I expected to make that a reality. Then I created all the action steps and automated everything, including reminders to make personal touches. You can't automate a personal touch, but you can automate the reminder to make that touch.

Don't Forget the Personal Touch

The more personal touches you have in your system, the better the experience will be for your client and anyone who works with you, including YOU! You really can have fun and get five times more business just by ramping up the personal touches in your business and automating them, so they take place even when you feel over-whelmed. Follow the system, and you won't be running around with your pants on fire all the time.

I created action plans inside my contact management system (many people call this a database) for every aspect of my business. We have built plans into our business specifically designed for our co-op agents, so they have an incredible experience when they cooperate on a sale with us. I have plans to remind me to post on social media and plans to remind me to lead-generate every day and grow my business by feeding the database every day. Each plan is customized to the people I currently have working on our team to help them stay accountable and deliver the world-class service my clients and I expect.

The most exciting thing that came out of my "Perfect Process" was the ability to create a simple, turnkey process for an instant job description, and a policy and procedure system to ensure we are delivering a world-class experience for everyone in the transaction. Everyone from me, my team, our clients, the co-op agent, their client, the title company, inspector, appraiser, lender and any others in the path of this real estate transaction tornado. We want them to feel as though they are hanging out in the eye of the storm without getting caught in the turbulent winds. When everyone around you trusts you and knows that working with you is easy, it makes everything else run so much more smoothly.

Establish an Annual Planning Session

One reminder from E-Myth is that a business is constantly evolving. Every year we have an annual planning session to create our "Perfect Processes" in line with the current people on our team. Everyone documents everything they do for two weeks. At the same time, I document everything I think they are doing. Once I get that list from everyone, I look over my list and cross off the duplicates.

The remaining items on my list is where all my frustration is coming from. It is possible they never understood why I needed that action step, or that they were the one accountable for completing that step.

When the entire team comes together and creates the perfect process, they see how everyone on the team intertwines to create the standards that deliver our ultimate experience. We discuss action items as a group to understand why each step is important in the overall experience the team or agent wants to deliver. By creating this process together, we can decide that certain steps in the process are not important, or that there might be a better way to get the result the team wants.

Your perfect process represents the core systems responsible for making your business vision, A-plus paper a reality. When you can convert your business into an assembly line that creates a real estate transaction with the predictability of a McDonald's hamburger, one where what you want and what you get are the same every time, you have begun to create an E-Myth-type business that is scalable and saleable, just like the millions of McDonald's franchises. If you want to create a Ritz-Carlton type experience, you must control every part of the transaction, and you will have to rely on other people. One person can't give every client a Ritz-Carlton experience. Automating your procedures and building your client expectations into that system will give you relief and the freedom to focus on their experience versus being the technician managing and micromanaging every step of the process.

The system I have shared with you will put accountability into your business and allow you to manage day-to-day activities, so you can create a bigger vision for your business, everyone who works with you and—most importantly—deliver an extraordinary experience to your clients.

As you will see in the next chapter, Michael has many insights to share about *management*. ✤

CHAPTER

7

On the Subject
of Management

Michael E. Gerber

The most important figures that one needs for management are unknown
or unknowable, but successful management must nevertheless take
account of them.

—W. Edwards Deming

E very real estate agent, including Steve Walsh from our story,
eventually faces the issue of management. Most face it badly.
 Why do so many real estate agents suffer from a kind of
paralysis when it comes to management? Why are so few able to get
their real estate business to work the way they want it to and run it on
time? Why are their managers (if they have any) seemingly so inept?

There are two main problems. First, the real estate agent
usually abdicates accountability for management by hiring an office
manager. Thus, the real estate agent is working hand in glove with
someone who is supposed to do the managing. But the real estate
agent is unmanageable himself!

The real estate agent doesn't think like a manager because he doesn't think he is a manager. He's a real estate agent! He rules the roost. And so he gets the office manager to take care of stuff like scheduling appointments, keeping his calendar, collecting receivables, hiring/firing, and much more.

Second, no matter who does the managing, they usually have a completely dysfunctional idea of what it means to manage. Everyone in a small, and hopefully growing, company tries to manage people instead of what really needs to be managed . . . The *systems* that, ideally, their people use to produce company results.

We often hear that a good manager must be a "people person." Someone who loves to nourish, figure out, support, care for, teach, baby, monitor, mentor, direct, track, motivate, and, if all else fails, threaten or beat up her people.

Don't believe it. Management has far less to do with people than you've been led to believe.

In fact, despite the claims of every management book written by management gurus (who have seldom managed anything), no one—with the exception of a few bloodthirsty tyrants—has ever learned how to manage people.

And the reason is simple: *People are almost impossible to manage.*

Yes, it's true. People are unmanageable. They're inconsistent, unpredictable, unchangeable, unrepentant, irrepressible, and generally impossible.

Doesn't knowing this make you feel better?

Now you understand why you've had all those problems! Do you feel the relief, the heavy stone lifted from your chest?

The time has come to fully understand what management is really all about. Rather than managing *people*, management is really all about managing a *process*, a step-by-step way of doing things that, combined with other processes, becomes a system. For example:

- The Process for on-time scheduling
- The Process for answering the telephone

- The Process for greeting a client
- The Process for organizing client files

Thus, a process is the step-by-step way of doing something over time. Considered as a whole, these processes are a system:

- The On-time Scheduling System
- The Telephone Answering System
- The Client Greeting System
- The File Organization System

Instead of managing people, then, the truly effective manager has been taught a *System* for managing a *Process* through which *People* get things done.

More precisely, managers and their people, *together,* manage the processes—the Systems—that comprise your business. Management is less about *who* gets things done in your business than about *how* things get done.

In fact, great managers are not fascinated with people, as our contemporary mantra suggests we must be, but instead, with how things get done through people using extraordinarily effective Systems to do it.

To do that, great managers constantly ask themselves and their people key questions, such as:

- What is the result we intend to produce?
- Are we producing that result every single time?
- If we're not producing that result every single time, why not?
- If we are producing that result every single time, how could we produce even better results?
- Do we lack a System? If so, what would that System look like if we were to create it?
- If we *have* a System, why aren't we using it?

And so forth.

In short, a great manager can leave the office fully assured it will run at least as well as it does when he or she is physically in the room.

Great managers are those who use a great management system. A system that shouts, "This is *how* we manage here." Not "This is *who* manages here."

In a truly effective company, how you manage is always more important than who manages. Provided a system is in place, how you manage is transferable, whereas who manages isn't. *How* you manage can be taught, whereas *who* manages can't be.

When a company is dependent on *who* manages—Katie, Kim, or Kevin—that business is in serious jeopardy. Because when Katie, Kim, or Kevin leaves, that business has to start over again. What an enormous waste of time and resources!

Even worse, when a company is dependent on *who* manages, you can bet all the managers in that business are doing their own thing. What could be more unproductive than ten managers who each manage in their unique way? How in the world could you possibly manage those managers?

The answer is: You can't. Because it takes you right back to trying to manage *people* again.

And, as I hope you now know, that's impossible.

In this chapter, I often refer to managers in the plural. I know that most real estate agents only have one manager, if they have one at all: the office manager. So you may be thinking a management system isn't so important in a small real estate business. You may be thinking a management system isn't so important in a small company, like a sole proprietorship. After all, the office manager is supposed to be doing whatever an office manager is supposed to do (and thank God, because you don't want to do it). Why go through the trouble of creating a Management System?

But if your company is ever going to turn into the business it could become, and if that business is ever going to turn into the enterprise of your dreams, then the questions you ask about how the office manager manages your affairs are critical ones. Because until you come to grips with your dual role as owner and key employee, and the relationship your manager has to those two roles, your company/business/enterprise will never realize its potential. Thus the need for a Management System.

Management System

What, then, is a Management System?

The E-Myth says a Management System is the method by which every manager innovates, quantifies, orchestrates, and then replicates the Systems through which your company produces the results you expect.

According to the E-Myth, a manager's job is simple: *a manager's job is to invent the Systems through which the owner's vision is consistently and faithfully manifested at the operating level of the business.*

Which brings us right back to the purpose of your business and the need for an entrepreneurial vision.

Are you beginning to see what I'm trying to share with you? That your business is *one single thing?* And that all the subjects we're discussing here—money, planning, management, and so on—are all about doing one thing well?

That one thing is the one thing your company is intended to do: distinguish your real estate business from all others on the planet.

It is the manager's role to make certain it all fits. And it's your role as entrepreneur to make sure your manager knows what the business is supposed to look, act, and feel like when it's finally done. As clearly as you know how, you must convey to your manager what you know to be true—your vision, your picture of the business when it's finally done. In this way, your vision is translated into your manager's marching orders every day he or she reports to work.

Unless that vision is embraced by your manager, you and your people will suffer from the tyranny of routine. And your business will suffer from it, too.

Now let's move on to *people*. Because, as we know, it's people who are causing all our problems. But before we do, let's read what Brad has to say about *management*. ✤

CHAPTER

8

Nothing Slips Through the Cracks

Brad Korn

Organize around business functions, not people. Build systems within each business function. Let systems run the business and people run the systems. People come and go but the systems remain constant.
—Michael Gerber, *The E-Myth Revisited: Why Most Small Businesses Don't Work and What to Do About It*

One of the main points Michael E. Gerber made in *The E-Myth* was to have a system that creates an extraordinary experience using ordinary people. I can't emphasize this enough. When I started out in real estate, I didn't know what an extraordinary level of service was. Real estate school doesn't teach that: it teaches the basics needed to pass the test and become a licensed real estate agent. The school's main responsibility is to cover laws and contracts, and get us all familiar with real estate jargon. Schools are not responsible for teaching new agents how to run a profitable real estate business or how to market listings to ensure the most exposure to get your client top dollar.

Did you know over half of all properties listed in MLS systems expire (don't sell in the first six months), given most market conditions? That means over half of agents' properties are not sold because they are not priced right, based on the property location or condition.

I would argue that those agents don't have a great marketing system to make sure the property gets sufficient exposure, and they don't have a system to help the seller get to the right price. Again, not their fault, because they were not taught market positioning. There is no secret pricing formula for agents to ensure they get it right, and there aren't any classes that teach agents how to negotiate detailed contracts. The three most critical things I wish I had been taught in the beginning of my real estate career are marketing, pricing strategies, and negotiating tactics.

There is a lot to learn when starting out in the real estate business, far more than they teach you in school. When I first started, I was overwhelmed trying to organize all the information in a constructive manner. As I learned more and more about everything that needed to happen to run a successful real estate business, I realized I needed a way to manage all of it and manage me to make sure it was getting done.

Automate Your Checklist

What is the transaction management system that takes place from the time a contract is accepted until it closes? I have a list of everything that needs to be done, plus the ninety-nine things that can go wrong from contract to close. Having an automated plan that keeps me accountable for getting things done when they need to get done gives me the freedom to deal with any of the ninety-nine things that can go wrong.

When I first started selling real estate, no one gave me a list or a system that would notify me of everything that needed to be done. Even if someone had given me a list, I would have had to look at that list every day, until the contract closed, to know if I had missed anything. That takes time and creates a reactive working environment. What about the time I had three or four contracts all going at once? The reason most agents can't close one hundred sales per year is because they work too hard trying to keep track of all the transactions going on simultaneously.

The system I created to overcome that obstacle shows me what tasks on the checklist are due each day, and I don't have to worry about what is on the list for tomorrow until tomorrow. A paper checklist puts people in reactive mode more than an automated accountability system that puts your next task in front of you every day. On top of that, I still have to manage to get more listings, call back the buyers who inquire about my listings, process paperwork, pay the bills, write ads to get more business, find the right affiliates, find products and services to make my life easier—the list goes on and on. It's no wonder 60 percent of all real estate agents don't make it past two years in the industry.

Fortunately for me, I was smart enough to read *The E-Myth Revisited* and began to implement systems to help me manage my business. I had to get a lot of listings if I wanted to stay in a commission-only business. If I was going to apply my ninety-nine-item checklist to every transaction, I had to have a bulletproof system to make sure nothing slipped through the cracks. There was no room for error. I could not raise my three daughters on a roller-coaster income.

I knew I had to get a consistent three to five closings every month and carry twenty-five to thirty listings at any given time. Keep in mind, it took me ten years to determine what these minimum numbers needed to be. Those numbers are much larger when there are people on the team with salaries and commission splits—and don't forget about personal and family needs. At one point, two of my girls were attending college at a major university at the same time. That meant six years of college tuition, books, and living expenses.

That is why you must have a management system for every level of your team. New agents don't have ten closings their first month out of real estate school, nor do they know where to go to get that kind of business. And top-selling agents at the top of their game easily forget about the things that got them where they are today. Once success happens, they hire people to do all the things they don't like to do. They get comfortable about where their business is. They don't have to do the little things they did every day, consistently, that got them to that point. They hired someone else to do all those little things.

But there's a problem unless that top-selling agent has a management system in place to ensure little things don't slip through the cracks. Eventually, those top sellers want to give up everything. Then they get frustrated that things are not getting done because the people they hired most likely did not invest time, like the real estate agent did, to figure out how to do it the best way. They haven't done the day-to-day, consistent activities to become "top of their game," and they don't know how to sustain the success.

Don't Reinvent the Wheel

There is hope, however. When successful agents can document the processes that made them successful and create a system around that, they can begin to experience what E-Myth is all about. The good news is you don't have to wait years to have a team to create your perfect processes. If you are brand-new to real estate and you put another top agent's system in place, then set it up to hold you accountable to do what that agent did, you will increase your chances of being the next superstar in your market. I shadowed and watched many of the top real estate agents in the industry and took notes while doing so. I rebuilt their systems—with my own personal touch—to create my perfect process.

The perfect processes will comprise your management system, and that system will include every aspect of your business. You'll want an automated system that holds everyone accountable and ensures that everything gets done without anything slipping through the cracks. Be sure you keep in mind the three core E-Myth focus points to perfect and bulletproof your system: innovation, quantification, and orchestration.

The hardest part of "E-Mythizing" your business is setting up the systems. But once you've created the systems, all you have to do is tweak them until you get the results you want every time. As your business grows and you continue to innovate, quantify, and orchestrate, you will see your real estate practice become a business—a business that operates on autopilot as it grows bigger than you ever imagined.

Perfect Your Systems BEFORE Hiring

As your business grows and you add people, you want to make sure whoever oversees your lead-capture and conversion systems continually quantifies the results. If you don't get the results you need to make a profit, you should tweak your systems to get the results you want. This will determine how successful your business will be.

When you run your systems through these three core focus points, your business will grow, and your client fulfillment systems will get better and better. In the People section you will find out more about getting buy-in from your team, and taking them through the innovation, quantification, and orchestration process. When perfected, your systems will deliver an extraordinary experience to your clients, your team, and everyone else involved, and they will be excited to a part of it with you.

So, the question is, how accountable are you to yourself? How accountable will you be to your own system? In real estate, most of us start out as one agent, and then grow to need an assistant and possibly more people to help us show properties and list more properties. For me in the beginning, when I realized I was the Technician and wanted to move to Manager and then Entrepreneur, I always said to myself, "How can I expect someone else to do things at the level I expect if I can't do them myself?"

I started my perfect process system when I was just one agent. That system allowed me to get to forty-five to seventy-five sales per year before I needed to expand my team. Today those systems are refined enough that an agent can get to seventy-five to one hundred sales per year as a solo agent—and could even get 125 to 150 sales with one assistant. In fact, the new world of real estate will have more and more agents doing 500, 1,000, even 3,000 sales per year with a well-oiled system.

Don't hire people before you perfect your systems. You'll go CRAZY, and your business won't be as profitable as it could be.

As Michael says, "The system does the work; the people work the system." Your management system is what ensures your people are accountable. If you build your business on a people-driven system, your business and success will depend on your people. People are unpredictable, and a people-driven business is an unpredictable business model.

Your System Becomes Your Personal Assistant

Think of your client fulfillment system and your perfect process system as your first hire. The system will be your first employee. If you run your system, the system will serve as your personal assistant. That first assistant is there to get you focused on the activities that will grow your business—and you won't have to pay someone a salary. Until you hire that first real person, the system keeps you focused on the dollar activities.

At first the system won't make all the non-dollar-productive activities go away. The daily busywork will still be there. That leverage to get your focus off the busy stuff and more on the dollar-productive activities will help you bring in new business, more income, and then hire a real person to take all the non-dollar activities off your plate. It is difficult to cross that bridge from Technician to Manager and get on the path to become a true business owner because we have a tendency to hire people before we have the money available. Most business owners hire people praying they will do enough of the right work to bring in enough income to pay for themselves.

Hiring people is scary! You are now responsible for another mouth to feed, and in turn, feeding their family. They rely on that paycheck or commission check so they can survive. Also, most Technicians are so busy doin' it, doin' it, doin' it that they don't have extra cash to cover an employee's salary. The technician typically will hire out of necessity when their business is spinning out of control and they didn't have a money system in place to get extra profit socked away to help make the next hire. When you create your perfect process, automate the process, and manage yourself through that process to be more efficient, you will free up time to grow your business. You will create the additional income to cover the salary of the new hire.

One of the first steps in the process is to get your client fulfillment systems in place. Write down what makes doing business with you so great, and get your system documented. Put it into an automated system that will manage you, even though you naturally deliver that great service. You want to have a system holding you accountable to the things you do best and prompting your clients to want to work with you. When your standards are documented and put into an action plan that happens, without fail, you will be ready to leverage yourself with people.

Now let's take a look at what Michael teaches us about *people* in the next chapter. ❖

CHAPTER

9

On the Subject of People

Michael E. Gerber

When you innovate, you've got to be prepared for people telling you that you are nut.

— Larry Ellison, founder of Oracle Corporation

Every real estate agent I've ever met has complained about people. About employees: "They come in late, they go home early; they have the focus of an antique camera!"

About mortgage lenders: "They're living in a non-parallel universe!"

About clients: "They want to buy a mansion on a town-home budget!"

People, people, people. Every real estate agent's nemesis. And at the heart of it all are the people who work for you.

"By the time I tell them how to do it, I could have done it twenty times myself!" "How come nobody listens to what I say?" "Why is it nobody ever does what I ask them to do?"

Does this sound like you?

So what's the problem with people? To answer that, think back to the last time you walked into a real estate agent's office. What did you see in the people's faces?

Most people working in real estate are harried. You can see it in their expressions. They're negative. They're bad-spirited. They're humorless. And with good reason. After all, they're surrounded by people who need a home, can't qualify for a loan, or can't get their offers accepted. Clients are looking for nurturing, for empathy, for care. And many are either terrified or depressed. They don't want to be there.

Is it any wonder employees at most real estate agencies are disgruntled? They're surrounded by unhappy people all day. They're answering the same questions 24/7. And most of the time, the real estate agent has no time for them. He or she is too busy leading a dysfunctional life.

Working with people brings great joy—and monumental frustration. And so it is with real estate agents and their people. But why? And what can we do about it?

Let's look at the typical real estate agent—who this person is and isn't.

Most real estate agents are unprepared to use other people to get results. Not because they can't find people, but because they are fixated on getting the results themselves. In other words, most real estate agents are not the businesspeople they need to be, but *technicians suffering from an entrepreneurial seizure*.

Am I talking about you? What were you doing before you became an entrepreneur?

Were you a corporate executive working for a large, multilocation organization? A midsized company? A small company?

Didn't you imagine owning your own company as the way out?

Didn't you think that because you knew how to do the technical work—because you knew so much about listings, research, sales screening, and property management—that you were automatically prepared to create a company that does that type of work?

Didn't you figure that by creating your own company, you could dump the boss once and for all? How else to get rid of that impossible person, the one driving you crazy, the one who never let you do your own thing, the one who was the main reason you decided to take the leap into a business of your own in the first place?

Didn't you start your own company so you could become your own boss?

And didn't you imagine that once you became your own boss, you would be free to do whatever you wanted to do—and to take home *all* the money?

Honestly, isn't that what you imagined? So you went into business for yourself and immediately dived into work.

Doing it, doing it, doing it.

Busy, busy, busy.

Until one day you realized (or maybe not) that you were doing all of the work. You were doing everything you knew how to do, plus a lot more you knew nothing about. Building sweat equity, you thought.

In reality, a technician suffering from an entrepreneurial seizure.

You were just hoping to make a buck in your own company. And sometimes you did earn a wage. But other times you didn't. You were the one signing the checks, all right, but they went to other people.

Does this sound familiar? Is it driving you crazy?

Well, relax, because we're going to show you the right way to do it this time.

Read carefully. Be mindful of the moment. You are about to learn the secret you've been waiting for all your working life.

The People Law

It's critical to know this about the working life of real estate agents who own their own real estate business: *Without people, you don't own a company, you own a job.* And it can be the worst job in the world because you're working for a lunatic! (Nothing personal—but we've got to face facts.)

Let me state what every real estate agent knows: Without people, you're going to have to do it all yourself. Without human help, you're doomed to try to do too much. This isn't a break-through idea, but it's amazing how many real estate agents ignore the truth. They end up knocking themselves out ten to twelve hours a day. They try to do more, but less actually gets done.

The load can double you over and leave you panting. In addition to the work you're used to doing, you may also have to do the books. And the organizing. And the filing. You have to do the planning and the scheduling. When you own your own company, the daily minutiae are never-ceasing—as I'm sure you've found out. Like painting the Golden Gate Bridge, it's endless. Which puts it beyond the realm of human possibility. Until you discover how to get it done by somebody else, it will continue on and on until you're a burned-out husk.

But with others helping you, things will start to drastically improve. If, that is, you truly understand how to engage people in the work you need them to do. When you learn how to do that, when you learn how to replace yourself with other people—people trained in your system—then your company can really begin to grow. Only then will you begin to experience true freedom yourself.

What typically happens is that real estate agents, knowing they need help answering the phone, filing, and so on, go out and find people who can do these things. Once they delegate these duties, however, they rarely spend any time with the employee. Deep down they feel it's not important how these things get done; it's only important that they get done.

They fail to grasp the requirement for a system that makes people their greatest asset rather than their greatest liability. A system so reliable that if Chris dropped dead tomorrow, Leslie could do exactly what Chris did. That's where the People Law comes in.

The People Law says that each time you add a new person to your company using an intelligent (turnkey) system that works, you expand your reach. And you can expand your reach almost infinitely! People allow you to be everywhere you want to be simultaneously, without actually having to be there in the flesh.

People are to a real estate agent what a record was to Frank Sinatra. A Sinatra record could be (and still can be) played in a million places at the same time, regardless of where Frank was. And every record sale produced royalties for Sinatra (or his estate).

With the help of other people, Sinatra created a quality recording that faithfully replicated his unique talents, then made sure it was marketed and distributed, and the revenue managed.

Your people can do the same thing for you. All you need to do is to create a "recording"—a system—of your unique talents, your special way of practicing real estate, and then replicate it, market it, distribute it, and manage the revenue.

Isn't that what successful businesspeople do? Make a "recording" of their most effective ways of doing business? In this way, they provide a turnkey solution to their clients' problems. A system solution that really works.

Doesn't your company offer the same potential for you that records did for Sinatra (and now for his heirs)? The ability to produce income without having to go to work every day.

Isn't that what your people could be for you? The means by which your system for practicing real estate could be faithfully replicated?

But first you have to have a system. You have to create a unique way of doing business that you can teach to your people, that you can manage faithfully, and that you can replicate consistently, just like McDonald's.

Because without such a system, without such a "recording," without a unique way of doing business that really works, all you're left with is people doing their own thing. And that is almost always a recipe for chaos. Rather than guarantee consistency, it encourages mistake after mistake after mistake.

And isn't that how the problem started in the first place? People doing whatever they perceived *they* needed to do, regardless of what you wanted? People left to their own devices, with no regard for the costs of their behavior. The costs to you.

In other words, people without a system.

Can you imagine what would have happened to Frank Sinatra if he had followed that example? If every one of his recordings had been done differently? Imagine a million different versions of "My Way." It's unthinkable.

Would you buy a record like that? What if Frank were having a bad day? What if he had a sore throat?

Please hear this: The People Law is unforgiving. Without a systematic way of doing business, people are more often a liability than an asset. Unless you prepare, you'll find out too late which ones are which.

The People Law says that without a specific system for doing business; without a specific system for recruiting, hiring, and training your people to use that system; and without a specific system for managing and improving your systems, your company will always be a crapshoot.

Do you want to roll the dice with your company at stake? Unfortunately, that is what most real estate agents are doing.

The People Law also says that you can't effectively delegate your responsibilities unless you have something specific to delegate. And that something specific is a way of doing business that works!

Sinatra is gone, but his voice lives on. And someone is still counting his royalties. That's because Sinatra had a system that worked.

Do you?

Now we will move on to the subject of *team members*. But before that, let's see what Brad has to say about *advisors*. ❖

CHAPTER
10

A Business Model So Simple Anyone Can Do It

Brad Korn

The system isn't something you bring to the business. It's something you derive from the process of building the business.
—Michael E. Gerber, *The E-Myth Revisited: Why Most Small Businesses Don't Work and What to Do About It*

A big challenge in any business is going from Technician to Manager and/or Entrepreneur. A successful business will have a profit. What no one really talks about in real estate is the low margin of profit. Don't be fooled by the big commission checks. A business owner looks at profit margins. You might have thought twice about getting into real estate if you knew what 90 percent of real estate agents' and real estate companies' profit margins are. By the time you factor in everyone who gets a piece of your commission—the broker, the coop agent—as well as any concessions you give, and all the expenses of running a real estate business, the true profit dwindles quickly.

If you are lucky enough to be in a market where the average price point is in the millions, it might be easier to add employees when you feel overwhelmed. However, you are most likely giving away thousands of dollars you don't need to spend.

Your business may not be able to sustain the lifestyle you're accustomed to. I started my real estate career in the Midwest where the average price point was around the $150,000 range. Many agents in other markets, like San Diego, were making millions of dollars and only selling twenty homes a year. How much were they working if they were only closing two houses a month? This book should give every real estate agent the systems to close as many as 75 to 125 sales per year without a big team of people. The systems are like having a $50,000-a-year, salaried key administrative hire. If someone already has a real estate team, each agent on the team should be able to close 75 to 125 sales each by using the systems in this book.

In the beginning of my career, I was stressed about money. By the time I got through real estate school, paid all the fees to get access to the MLS, lockbox keys, signs, I had spent a lot more money than I had planned to. Not to mention the marketing I was going to have to do to get my name out there.

Do Only What You Love to Do

Running a real estate business is a lot like opening a brick-and-mortar business in your local downtown area. You have to make a large investment upfront so people will know about you and do business with you. During my first three years of real estate in Minnesota, no one knew me. It was difficult, and I had to do a lot of extra work I didn't enjoy. Thanks to Michael and the E-Myth books, I set up systems to automate a lot of the mundane, critical tasks that every business on the planet has to do, efficiently knocking that stuff off my "to do" list. That way, I was doing only the stuff I love to do. If you are happy in your job, you will attract happy clients and happy people who want to work with you, and you will have happy agents in your office. The reverse will happen if you are doing a job you think is overly tedious and not enjoyable. You will not attract the agents or the clients you want to work with.

Today you might hear me say, "I must be cheating the system because I really don't feel like I am working that hard to close one hundred transactions per month." The reality is, I love what I do, and I focus on what I love to do. Of course, there are days when I don't feel like listing a house, but I do it so I can continue to pursue a job I love and get paid for it. What makes it work are the systems. In the next couple of chapters, we will talk about the E-Myth principle of "Estimating." That means I know exactly how long it will take me to get that appointment done. I don't worry about wasting time driving over and finding out the sellers are not home, or wondering if they are going to keep me there longer than expected. I have a process I follow that works nearly every single time.

I set up my systems to track and hold accountable every person who works with me and my clients. Because whenever something goes wrong in a real estate transaction, the client blames the real estate agent. It doesn't matter if it was the agent's fault or if someone else involved in the transaction was to blame. As political strategist Lee Atwater said, "Perception is reality." Clients don't always tell you when they are upset or feel like you dropped the ball. Instead, they disappear and never call back. I wanted to stop the false accusations and plug the holes by orchestrating a better system.

Throughout my systems are built-in "check-in" points, especially when part of the transaction is out of my control. I contact everyone involved to find out the status of their part of the transaction because this is my client, and I want him or her to have a great experience with me. We never bother our clients with all the unimportant issues that come up from the lender, title company, appraiser, inspector, termite abatement, the other agent, or the other party in the transaction. They know this, they expect it, and that is why they choose us. My systems are set up so that everyone's job in the transaction is in my system, which helps us make sure it gets done. My goal is for every person involved—from the consumer to the coop agent, affiliates, and the people on my team—to have a great experience. When you have happy people around you, you have a happy business.

Nothing Slips Through the Cracks

A proven, automated system allows us to take care of all the predictable things without anything slipping through the cracks. Because we are human, we forget things. Each of us has a million things running through our head all day long: things you forgot to do yesterday, what you want for lunch, and a reminder to pick up the dry cleaning on the way home. And then, "Oh shoot, I forgot to call what's-his-name." We do have bad days, and we lose focus. If you just "wing it" or use your experience to get you through, you will quickly find that any given day in the real estate industry is unpredictable.

When a system is running, it can pull you back on track and get back to the predictable side of real estate.

The real estate industry doesn't make it easy to have an E-Myth-type business where you can easily give your clients a WOW! experience. Few other businesses have potential outcomes as devastating as those in real estate. Your clients can find out the day of closing that it is not happening. Their moving truck could be in the parking lot at the title/escrow/attorney's office, and their plans had called for sleeping in their new home that night. Everyone else in the transaction—including the lender, title person, attorney, and agents—will all go home to their families tonight and sleep in their own bed. That poor consumer must scramble to find a hotel room, stay with relatives, or go back to their old, empty house and sleep on the floor without utilities. These are real people, and when they have an experience like this, they never want to move again. This is the last house they will ever buy. That doesn't do a whole lot of good for the industry. All my systems revolve around preventing these things from happening, and our clients are aware of issues before they happen so they are not caught off guard.

Everybody in the transaction is important. I know my team members feel bad for our clients when things fall through. Sometimes they can't sleep at night when they know our client is having a bad experience. I set up all our systems for everyone. You want to keep the good and great people on your team around for a long time. Our systems give them the opportunity to experience the same thing I do: enjoying life, loving what they do. Our systems help give them the lifestyle they want, the opportunity to make a satisfying income, or the flexibility to be with their kids as they grow up. Every system runs through the same filter: if I am not having fun, the system is broken. I won't do something that isn't fun, and our clients need to have a fun experience as well. If we are having fun, they will have fun, refer friends and family to us, and do business with us again in the future.

The great thing about following my *The E-Myth Real Estate Agent* business model is that your business gets to grow into a big business over time. Your systems will grow and improve while you are growing. You don't just dump it all in place and hire twenty, fifty, one thousand employees and start selling one thousand homes tomorrow. You will move to that Zen spot of balancing your technician, manager, and entrepreneur to ultimately give consumers an incredible experience. So many businesses want to build it all and then wait for the people to show up. It never worked that way for me, and I have seen way too many real estate agents go out of business or lose everything they had because they didn't get the business principles we are talking about here.

So, when you begin the process of looking for people to join your real estate business, searching for vendors and affiliates to align yourself with, and finding the clients who are fun to work with and listen to your advice, it will come back to how you are feeling. Are you happy? Are you having fun? If you find yourself doin' it, doin' it, doin' it every day, day in and day out and not getting ahead, you can burn out. You can stop attracting fun people. The systems allow you not to get lost in the "doin' it every day," get focused and accountable to do the right things more, and get the mundane tasks off your list.

Real estate is a dangerous business because you don't have to sell a lot of homes to make a comfortable, better-than-average income. Think about it: if you sell twelve homes a year and your average commission is $5,000, you will bring in a gross income of $60,000. Now, what you will realize is that a lot of people seem to want their share of your commission. You can spend around 50 percent to 60 percent of your gross commission just to run a real estate business. If your overall expenses are less than 30 percent to 40 percent of your gross income, you might not be leveraging your money to get the most out of your commission dollars. The point here is that someone living in a high-end market could be making a $30,000 commission. If they sell just sell ten homes a year, their gross could be $300,000, netting them $150,000 to $200,000. The question is, how can you master selling real estate, marketing, negotiating, and pricing homes right if you only do it once a month?

Don't Get Stuck on the Hamster Wheel

I do realize that a lot of people are not like me. They might thrive on having a to-do list every day. But I suspect they have not done their A+ paper. They have not gone "beyond the E-Myth" to create a BIG vision of what could be, and then built their current business into that big vision. They might get stuck on the hamster wheel forever and never be able to dream big and go big. I know if I had to come in every day and chunk away at a to-do list of everything that needed to be done, including stuff I hate doing, I would quit doing it and, eventually, quit real estate entirely.

If you feel like you just are barely surviving and not getting the results you want, sit down with a blank sheet of paper. Paint a picture of what you would like to have, then start doing something different than you are doing right now to move in the direction of that vision. Plenty of people have horrible experiences in real estate, both agents and consumers. Come from the mind-set that if you don't find your vision, you won't change the experience for you or your clients. If you don't change the experience, either your clients won't do business with you, or you might decide to do something different, like get another job or join some team that makes big promises to feed you as many leads as you can handle. Beware: there are no greener pastures than what you can do for yourself and for your clients.

This chapter is about people.

So, the first and most important thing you can do to implement change is to find more people. What I mean by that is more people who want to buy and sell real estate. It surprises me when I talk to real estate agents who have been in business for one year, two years or even five to ten years or more, and they only have one hundred, 200 or 400 people in their database. People are the key to your success. Every one of those agents has met more than that many people in his or her lifetime. They just aren't putting people in their system every day.

Every Person You Meet Is a Lead

One of the legs on the three-legged E-Myth stool is lead generation. Another leg is lead conversion. Remember that every person you meet is a lead. Really! The National Association of Realtors® tracks how often the average person moves. The average person moves every five to ten years. That means that 10 percent to 20 percent of the people you meet every day are going to be moving THIS YEAR. If you meet five people a day (buyers, sellers, or just regular people you bump into) and see them as potential leads in the next five or ten years, you would capture those five people a day and put them in your lead conversion system. If you did that five days a week for a month, you would add one hundred people to your database that month. If you did that for twelve months, you would add 1,200 people into your lead conversion system. Michael makes it very clear in his E-Myth books that if your business isn't growing, it is *dying!* Growing means adding people (capturing leads) to your database (lead conversion system) every day, every day, every day!

When you create the systems to capture and convert, you will realize that 1,200 people means that 120 to 240 people will be moving in the next year. If you add 1,200 people the second year, you will have a predictable 240 to 480 real estate sales opportunities the following year. When you get on purpose and do this simple thing—adding five people a day to your database—you will find out why you need an automated client fulfillment system that can hold an entire team of people accountable to deliver your world-class service and experience to your clients.

Now let's dive into another important topic and see what Michael has to say about *team members*. ❖

Meaningful relationships and meaningful work are mutually

On the Subject of Team Members

Michael E. Gerber

reinforcing, especially when supported by radical truth and radical transparency.

—Ray Dalio

If you're a sole practitioner—that is, you're selling only yourself—then your real estate business, called a *sole proprietorship*, will never make the leap to a real estate agency called a *business*. The progression from sole proprietorship to business to enterprise demands that you hire other real estate agents to do what you do (or don't do). Contractors call these people subcontractors; for our purposes, we'll refer to them as team members.

Contractors know that subs can be a huge problem. It's no less true for real estate agents. Until you face this special business problem, your company will never become a business, and your business will certainly never become an enterprise.

Long ago, God said, "Let there be real estate agents. And so they never forget who they are in my creation, let them be damned forever to hire people exactly like themselves." Enter the team members.

Solving the Team Member Problem

Let's say you're about to hire a team member. Someone who has specific skills: property management, buyer's agent, whatever. It all starts with choosing the right personnel. After all, these are people to whom you are delegating your responsibility and for whose behavior you are completely liable. Do you really want to leave that choice to chance? Are you that much of a gambler? I doubt it.

If you've never worked with your new associate, how do you know he or she is skilled? For that matter, what does "skilled" mean?

For you to make an intelligent decision about this team member, you must have a working definition of the word *skilled*. Your challenge is to know *exactly* what your expectations are, then make sure your other real estate agents operate with precisely the same expectations. Failure here almost assures a breakdown in your relationship.

I want you to write the following on a piece of paper: "By *skilled*, I mean . . ." Once you create your personal definition, it will become a standard for you and your company, for your clients, and for your team members.

A standard, according to *Merriam-Webster's Collegiate Dictionary, Eleventh Edition*, is something "set up and established by authority as a rule for the measure of quantity, weight, extent, value, or quality."

Thus, your goal is to establish a measure of quality control, a standard of skill, which you will apply to all your team members. More importantly, you are also setting a standard for the performance of your company.

By creating standards for your selection of other real estate agents—standards of skill, performance, integrity, financial stability, and experience—you have begun the powerful process of building a company that can operate exactly as you expect it to.

By carefully thinking about exactly what to expect, you have already begun to improve your company.

In this enlightened state, you will see the selection of your team members as an opportunity to define what you (1) intend to provide for your clients, (2) expect from your employees, and (3) demand for your life.

Powerful stuff, isn't it? Are you up to it? Are you ready to feel your rising power?

Don't rest on your laurels just yet. Defining those standards is only the first step you need to take. The second step is to create a *team member development system.*

A team member development system is an action plan designed to tell you what you are looking for in a team member. It includes the exact benchmarks, accountabilities, timing of fulfillment, and budget you will assign to the process of looking for team members, identifying them, recruiting them, interviewing them, training them, managing their work, auditing their performance, compensating them, reviewing them regularly, and terminating or rewarding them for their performance.

All of these things must be documented—actually *written down*— if they're going to make any difference to you, your team members, your managers, or your bank account!

And then you've got to persist with that system, come hell or high water. Just as Ray Kroc did. Just as Walt Disney did. Just as Sam Walton did.

This leads us to our next topic of discussion: the subject of *estimating.* But first, let's read what Brad has to say on the subject of *employees.* ❖

How to Get Buy-In from Everyone

Brad Korn

And what makes people work is an idea worth working for, along with a clear understanding of what needs to be done.
—Michael E. Gerber, *The E-Myth Revisited: Why Most Small Businesses Don't Work and What to Do About It*

The first time I read *The E-Myth Revisited* in my early days of real estate, something Michael E. Gerber said stuck out for me: "Talent is overrated." Talented people can help you build a big business. However, the talented people we might like to hire may be successful at what they are doing right now. Think about real estate. There are millions of real estate agents in the world, but only a handful have built a true real estate business that keeps growing after they step away from it.

What I mean by "grow" is that the business increases in size and volume significantly year after year, even when these top agents are involved in their business for only a few hours a week. As top agents, we think we need talented people like ourselves to be able to step out of the business. So we convince ourselves the person we've hired is the talented person we want so bad. Maybe we try to find them too soon in the process, or we don't talk to enough people to find the truly talented ones. If you don't want to be "in the trenches" every day and you find people just like yourself, don't you imagine they want the same thing you want?

But what happens when you build your business with a person who doesn't want to work that hard, and what if that person leaves before you find another person like you? Does it all end? Do you come back to work? I think everyone would love to skip the hard work and immediately emulate the lifestyle of top agents. A successful business runs like a machine. If you find an agent who has franchise-like systems you can buy, and that system gets the same results every time, you can take a shortcut. That is why the franchise business model is so successful. Those businesses are built on a system, not on people. The most successful franchise models work in any market, and they can hire just about anyone to come into their business and deliver predictable results and profits.

Let me say this a different way. Imagine you just had a remarkably profitable month. You worked hard. You got a big payday to reflect all that hard work. And then, on a whim, you decided, "I am going to take a day off, or even a week off." Heck, I know agents who take the last two months of the year off! If you build a people-driven business and your staff worked hard as well, is it possible you all would want that week off? If you are gone for a week or a month, will they work as hard as they did the previous month? I bet they all feel like they deserve that time off. Is there a system in place to keep everything going at the same pace, so you don't feel like you have to get away? What about your employees and team members? What if you had a system that took away the overwhelm, and your business ran smoothly whether you were closing two deals this month—or twenty deals?

I am not saying don't look for or hire talented people. Michael makes a great point throughout the E-Myth books that when you create an extraordinary system that delivers an unbelievable experience for the client—using ordinary people—you have created a business that can deliver what it promises. When you have a system that provides predictable results for ordinary people to deliver an extraordinary experience to your clients, you can grow your business with anyone who wants to be a part of your team. You will find a lot more ordinary people who want to work with you than extraordinary people. When people run great systems, the systems deliver extraordinary results from average people. Everyone on your team will deliver the experience you expect. When you find that talented person and plug him or her into that system, you will get superhero-like results.

If you have heard of Pareto's Principle (also known as the 80/20 rule), you can apply that to hiring people. Eighty percent of the people you hire will deliver 20 percent of the results you expect. Twenty percent of the people will deliver 80 percent of the results you expect. That means if you want five super, extra-talented people in your organization, you will have to interview people every day for the rest of your career. Think about it. If you want talent, you would have to interview 200 to 300 people to hire one hundred average people. On your quest to find the good people, you will need to fire at least eighty of the "average" people who don't work out. You would be left with twenty better-than-average people. Fifteen of those people will be just good enough that you won't want to fire them. However, they still may not be the "talent" you were looking for. You may only find them 5 percent of the time. And if you hired them in a batch of your 80 percent, and there are no systems to help them be extra successful, they may leave before you figure out they were the talented people you were looking for.

Talented people push you. They will require you to be more of the Entrepreneur, with a big enough vision to help them achieve everything they want. The five people who are "talent" from your pool of twenty above-average people will require more from you than you may have to give. When they have great systems to plug into that make them even better than they imagined, you will have the start of a business that can grow on its own.

Over the past twenty-five years, I personally have added about twenty-five people to my real estate team, which is never larger than eight people at one time. If I had to wait around for talent or, worse yet, go through eighty hires to find the talent, I would not have doubled my business year after year. I wouldn't have had time! I would have been interviewing, hiring, and firing people every day. I surely would not have been selling a consistent, predictable one hundred homes a year for over fifteen years—and most definitely would not have been writing this book with Michael.

Fortunately, you have this book to help you create all the systems to become one of the top 5 percenters in your area and not get stuck among the 60 percent to 80 percent who don't make it and get out of real estate. Think about it: there is no other opportunity like real estate where an average person without a business degree or any special skills has the opportunity to make millions of dollars and create whatever lifestyle he or she wants by fulfilling the biggest dream of all, homeownership. WOW! We have quite a responsibility.

Let's talk about bridging the gap between being just one agent to hiring your first employee, and eventually adding more team members. I find the majority of real estate agents are not excited about hiring people or managing people. In fact, people say to me all the time, "I don't want to run a BIG team like you do. That is more work than I want to do." The reality is, in the beginning my team was just me. Then it grew to two, then to three people, and we did one hundred sales! That is not a BIG team. Plus, with perfect process systems and accountability to *The E-Myth Real Estate Agent's* turnkey action plans, there isn't a lot of people management involved if the people on the team trust and use the systems. Your management system will hold people accountable for predictable results.

Another myth is that agents truly believe the client is doing business with *them* because of them. You have a business work ethic and a standard you live by, and that's why a client wants to work with you. That last part is true, but once that standard is documented, you can create your perfect client fulfillment system and automate it. That is when you will have duplicated yourself and your level of service to help more people. When your systems deliver your expected client, even using average people on your team, you increase your chances for higher profitability. The reality is, average people don't cost as much to hire as talented people.

This may be the biggest challenge you face before you can "E-Myth" your business. You see, you are going to have to do it differently than you are doing right now. Think of it as creating a new you, a new company—and continuing to run your old company as you innovate, quantify, and orchestrate your new company. Real estate is fun. If you already love what you do and are experiencing success, then sharing that "fun" with everyone around you will make it even more fun!

The bridge between where you are now and that next hire is a scary bridge to cross. Some agents just buy their way across the bridge. Others never cross the bridge. No matter where you are in your real estate business, whenever you reach that bridge, I challenge you to find a new and innovative way to cross it. Set up your people system to bring in enough new income so you can put away three months of projected salary before you make that first hire. If you create the system first, you should become more efficient and make an extra sale or two. Put that money aside in your new-hire salary fund. Now, when you find a new candidate to join your team, you will already have banked two to three months of their payroll. The same system that helped you get the extra sales will allow them to be productive right away and be an immediate asset, instead of an expense, to the team. As a rule, it's always best not to add a new expense without a plan to increase your profit by the amount of the expense. That means every team member should be able to produce a five- to ten-times return on what he or she is costing the team.

For most agents, hiring others means taking a step back from where you currently stand because of the time it takes to train new people. You also have to realize the new hire is not going to be as passionate about your business as you are. This is your baby. Even when real estate agents hire family, or their kids, those people didn't birth the business. They probably are not going to jump out of bed, excited to grow *your* business every day. I am here to tell you, if you don't have a guaranteed system for their success, they will not be up at night worrying about you. They will be up at night worrying about themselves. Eventually, they will leave for something they think is better or that they think they can do themselves.

The first step to hiring anyone is to get all your systems in place. To create this Perfect Process, you must track what you do every day. I will share my system for tracking time in Chapter 22. Once you have completed this exercise, you may find a lot of the action items and pieces of your perfect process right there. Then you can create your Perfect Process.

Once, I made the mistake of relying on our systems so strongly that I disappeared from my business for about eight months. I found a replacement for my role on the team, which allowed me to follow my passion to help other agents by speaking and training throughout the industry. The systems gave me the leverage to step out of the day-to-day business and document my systems so that, eventually, I could write this book to help agents get their lead generation, lead conversion and client fulfillment systems in place.

What I failed to do as a business owner was to build check-in points into the system so I could keep a pulse on my business. The system did work. While I was out of my business for that eight months, the system carried us to another predictable one hundred sales that year. However, what I soon found out was that "I" was the one "feeding the database" every day and had assumed the team would do the same. They didn't. During that eight months, they were benefiting from the residual results of the system I had been running for more than ten years. After ten months I found our listing inventory was the lowest it had been in that ten years.

Luckily, I noticed what was happening, stepped back into the team, and turned it around in three short months. Just by jumping back into the system and feeding it every day, we went from twenty listings (half of which were overpriced and not saleable) past our normal forty listings on up to sixty listings. And that's where our listing inventory remained for several years. That ramp-up was what set up our survival for the shift that was coming in the real estate market.

I can't stress enough how important it is for you to get systematized before you bring on a big team. As your team grows, you can improve and change the system to keep them accountable. Your management system will keep everyone focused on their tasks. Those systems will allow you to focus on your team members more to find out what is important to them. Help them reach their life goals, assist them with day-to-day struggles, and guide them in streamlining their part of the system so they don't get overworked and burned out.

If you are overwhelmed and think you need more team members, check your systems first. Your systems should make the job easy for you to handle. When you have systems that work, you can run your business on overwhelm for a short time and sock away three months of the potential new hire's salary or pay.

Once you have three months in the bank that you don't have to use, and it looks like you will have extra to cover the fourth month, you will be ready to plug a new hire into your system. This one tip changed the way I hire people. It gave me confidence in my systems and their ability to make us more productive. The training cycle can be drastically shortened, allowing new members of the team to enhance your business and bring value right away. When you plug someone into a system that allows them to do what they do best, they will deliver a higher level of predictable service to every client.

I hope I have inspired you to think about systems differently. I hope you are getting excited about what systems can do for your business right now. If you create systems for every aspect of your business, you can become more like a franchise. You will need a follow-up system for everyone on your team. Your management system should include personal touches to remind you to keep in touch with your team members and show them you care about them.

As the saying goes, "The greatest gift you can give someone is your time." It is easy to forget that the people you work with might look up to you for direction and advice. Create systems to help them get better at their roles. Create systems that make their roles easier and more predictable. Create systems that help them have guaranteed success at their role on the team. When your team members trust the system, they know what to expect, eliminating the unknown. When the unknown is gone, your people will be more confident in what they are doing and happier in their job. When you have happy people around you, you attract more happy people.

Now let's find out what Michael has to say about *estimating*. ✤

CHAPTER 13

On the Subject of Estimating

Michael E. Gerber

You can't manage what you can't measure.

—Peter Drucker

One of the greatest weaknesses of real estate agents is accurately estimating how long a sales job will take and then scheduling their sales accordingly. *Webster's Eleventh* defines estimate as "a rough or approximate calculation." Anyone who has bought or sold a house knows that those estimates can be rough indeed.

Do you want to see someone who gives you a rough approximation? What if your real estate agent gave you a rough approximation on the value of a property you are interested in?

The fact is that we can predict many things we don't typically predict. For example, there are ways to assess the market value of a house. Look at the steps of the process. Most of the things you do are standard, so develop a step-by-step system and stick to it.

In my book *The E-Myth Manager*, I raised eyebrows by suggesting that doctors eliminate the waiting room. Why? You don't need it if you're always on time. The same goes for a real estate business. If you're always on time, then your clients don't have to wait.

What if a real estate agent made this promise: on time, every time, as promised? "Impossible!" real estate agents cry. "Each client is different. We simply can't know how long each appointment will take."

Do you follow this? Since real estate agents believe they're incapable of knowing how to organize their time, they build a company based on lack of knowing and lack of control. They build a company based on estimates.

I once had a real estate agent ask me, "What happens when a distressed homeowner contacts us to sell his house, and we discover that its foundation needed to be repaired? How can we deal with that so unexpectedly?" My first thought was that it's not being dealt with now. Few real estate agents are able to give generously of their time. Ask anyone who's been to a real estate agent's office lately. It's chaos.

The solution is interest, attention, analysis. Try detailing what you do at the beginning of an interaction, what you do in the middle, and what you do at the end. How long does each take? Proper attention means anticipating mistakes or unexpected obstacles, and the time it takes to deal with them. In the absence of such detailed, quantified standards, everything ends up being an estimate, and a poor estimate at that.

However, a company organized around a system, with adequate staff to run it, has time for proper attention. It's built right into the system.

Too many real estate agents have grown accustomed to thinking in terms of estimates without thinking about what the term really means. Is it any wonder many real estate agencies are in trouble?

Enlightened real estate agents, in contrast, banish the word *estimate* from their vocabulary. When it comes to estimating, just say no!

"But you can never be exact," real estate agents have told me for years. "Close, maybe. But never exact."

I have a simple answer to that: You have to be. You simply can't afford to be inexact. You can't accept inexactness in yourself or in your real estate business.

You can't go to work every day believing that your company, the work you do, and the commitments you make are all too complex and unpredictable to be exact. With a mind-set like that, you're doomed to run a sloppy ship. A ship that will eventually sink and suck you down with it.

This is so easy to avoid. Sloppiness—in both thought and action—is the root cause of your frustrations.

The solution to those frustrations is clarity. Clarity gives you the ability to set a clear direction, which fuels the momentum you need to grow your business.

Clarity, direction, momentum—they all come from insisting on exactness.

But how do you create exactness in a hopelessly inexact world? The answer is this: You discover the exactness in your company by refusing to do any work that can't be controlled exactly.

The only other option is to analyze the market, determine where the opportunities are, and then organize your company to be the exact provider of the services you've chosen to offer.

Two choices, and only two choices: (1) evaluate your company, and then limit yourself to the tasks you know you can do exactly, or (2) start all over by analyzing the market, identifying the key opportunities in that market, and building a company that operates exactly.

What you cannot do, what you must refuse to do, from this day forward, is to allow yourself to operate with an inexact mind-set. It will lead you to ruin.

Which leads us inexorably back to the word I have been using throughout this book: *systems*.

Who makes estimates? Only real estate agents who are unclear about exactly how to do the task in question. Only real estate agents whose experience has taught them that if something can go wrong, it will—and to them!

I'm not suggesting that a *systems solution* will guarantee that you always perform exactly as promised. But I am saying that a systems solution will faithfully alert you when you're going off track, and will do it before you have to pay the price for it.

In short, with a systems solution in place, your need to estimate will be a thing of the past, both because you have organized your company to anticipate mistakes, and because you have put into place the system to do something about those mistakes before they blow up.

There's this, too: To make a promise you intend to keep places a burden on you and your managers to dig deeply into how you intend to keep it. Such a burden will transform your intentions and increase your attention to detail.

With the promise will come dedication. With dedication will come integrity. With integrity will come consistency. With consistency will come results you can count on. And results you can count on mean that you get exactly what you hoped for at the outset of your company: the true pride of ownership that every real estate agent should experience.

This brings us to the subject of *clients*. Who are they? Why do they come to you? How can you identify yours? And who *should* your clients be? But first, let's listen to what Brad has to say about *estimating* in your real estate business. ❧

CHAPTER 14

Make Every Real Estate Transaction Predictable

Brad Korn

A business that looks orderly says to your customer that your people know what they're doing.
—Michael E. Gerber, *The E-Myth Revisited: Why Most Small Businesses Don't Work and What to Do About* It

Let's talk about how much time it takes to *"do"* the real estate business. When a transaction is falling apart, it can consume you as you try to keep it together. We can lose hours or days just dealing with the issues. When a business operates in reactive mode, agents can find themselves working sixty-plus hours per week *"in"* their business and not working *"on"* their business.

If you assume the average full-time agent is closing two transactions per month and working forty to sixty hours per week, that is 240 hours per month. If they are closing two transactions per month, that would be 120 hours per closed transaction. What is wrong with this picture? Honestly, how long does it take to close one transaction? Surely it shouldn't take 120 hours, or two weeks of working sixty hours per week.

In my early days, I found myself consumed with a single transaction because I *needed* that transaction to close. It was one of my only "deals" that month, and I had bills to pay. If there was a chance of something going wrong with a transaction, I would spend an entire day to save one deal; it was income I needed and, if it fell apart, where else was I going to get the money to pay my bills? Turns out, I may have only spent about two to three hours physically working on saving it by leaving messages, talking to clients and agents, writing up solutions, etc. But my brain was preoccupied for the entire two days.

When systems are in place, you are free to spend more time on these things while your business continues to grow. Even with all the uncertainty of a real estate transaction, I promise you every transaction can have a predictable "estimating formula." Over the past twenty-plus years implementing and running systems, I've learned that just about every process in the real estate transaction can be systematized and controlled.

The process of going on a listing appointment is completely controllable. Agents might argue that certain sellers might ask more questions than others and, therefore, it's hard to anticipate how long an appointment will be. The truth is every business should be able to predict and systematize the time it takes for everything to happen. How long does it take to show one property, or ten properties? How long does a closing take? If you think these are not controllable, it may be because you are "winging it" and relying on your experience to get you through. Your expertise is not duplicable and scalable without a system. When you just let things happen is when real estate takes over your life and controls you.

If your time isn't predictable from appointment to appointment, you have not figured out your "perfect system." McDonald's has customers who special-order food all the time or might order ten times more than the previous person. Yet no matter what you order, you get your food fast. You want a McDonald's-like system for real estate. When you are successful and get referrals, the person who referred you told the referral client how great you are. They probably told them how great their experience was because you had a smooth transaction. Can you repeat that experience every time? If you are "winging it" in your business—even a little bit—and one detail slips through the cracks, that referral will tell their friend or family member that their experience was not like the one described. At that point, all referrals from that source will most likely stop. How predictable are your referrals? Without a referral process and system, your referrals will be random.

My listing appointments have been systematized and perfected to the McDonald's-like system. The appointment is time blocked on my calendar for the same time frame on every appointment. This gives me a controllable and predictable business, where I know I can handle up to five listing appointments every day. You can't sit around hoping your business will do better and grow; you must set up a system to make sure it does. When you accept that, even in real estate, the amount of time it takes to do every part of your business can be estimated, you will begin to control your business and surpass any goals you set in the past. When your business is a machine, it can double or triple at any level.

My systems were created for a one- to four-person team to get to three to four listing appointments in one day, five days a week. That would be fifteen to twenty listing appointments per week, every week, all year. With these tight goals, every appointment had to adhere to a strict schedule. Of course, some appointments may run shorter than predicted if the prequalifying questions show that a property can't sell right now. When that happens, we don't just drop the appointment. We still meet with them because we know they will be selling in the next one to five years. Every time we add new people to the sales funnel, our pipeline fills up. As it fills up over the next one to five years, the results our business produces will be more predictable.

The buyer process can be estimated as well. Our buyer consultation is just as predictable as our showing process. We can meet with a buyer, show them just a few homes, and write a contract in a set amount of time, every time. Understand that when I say this, we do not show buyers thirty, forty, sixty, or eighty homes. If McDonald's had a special-order burger that took one hour to make, the customer would have a bad experience and might never return. *The systems are created for the consumer!* Remember, they move every five to seven years, on average, so they don't always remember how the process goes, even if they are buying for a third or fourth time.

If you want the experience to be memorable and enjoyable, like going to Disneyland, then your Disney-like experience has to have a Disney-like system. I don't think Disney or McDonald's relies solely on a paper checklist system these days. They have not built systems dependent on the people to deliver their world-class experience. I recently heard McDonald's has a turnover rate of more than 300 percent. Yet you get the same thing, year after year, when you order food at McDonald's. Do your clients have a Disney experience every time they buy or sell a home with you? We can run buyers through our system five days a week, help twenty-five-plus buyers at any given time—and no one on the team feels like they are losing control as long as they use the system.

You need to know how long every process takes if you want to your team to do more business in less time. Without estimating, someone on the team could take five times longer to do the same activity you did. If you don't have a system in place, they will become over-whelmed and unable to handle more clients. Estimating will allow each person to specialize in their job responsibilities and become the most efficient they can be. As you develop an estimating formula for your real estate business, think of yourself as multiple people special-izing in one task at a time instead of one person specializing in all tasks all the time. When everyone specializes in one piece of the puzzle, they are going to be much more efficient than someone trying to be a "jack of all trades, master of none."

An example of estimating a piece of my business would be my seller market reviews. In a stable market, the average market time can vary. In my market, it could be a sixty or ninety days before we receive an offer on a market listing. Even in a stable market, two to four weeks can seem like an eternity for someone selling their home. The system I used for in-person seller market reviews resulted in nine out of ten price changes, and I knew I would only be there for fifteen minutes. We met with our sellers every two weeks. With my system, I knew I could meet with four sellers in one hour. That system led to more than $80,000 in price adjustments in less than an hour, and we helped those clients get their homes sold. That is what I call an efficient, successful day.

You conquer estimating when you create your step-by-step system for everything. Your listing process must ensure your client the most exposure to get the most money in the shortest amount of time. If your process to get the house on the market takes a month, a few weeks, one week, or even one whole day, you are missing out on buyers who might be willing to pay more now. If your process for listing is different on every property, your unpredictable system is costing your client. If you are waiting on photographers, sign companies, and anyone else to do their part before you make a listing "live," you might have lost a buyer who would have loved that house but settled for something else because your process took two to three days. You won't know if they would have offered more than asking price—a lost opportunity. Every day a property is not on the market while the agent is "getting it ready" is a lost opportunity. If those buyers buy something else in the meantime, they are gone forever, or at least for the next five to seven years.

If you truly want to stand behind a statement like "getting a client the most money possible in the shortest amount of time," then the time to be live on the market is the day your clients know they are moving. To build a predictable business, you will need to estimate and systematize your perfect listing process, so your client has an incredible, predictable experience. I believe no one should ever have to wait to get their house on the market. That's why I created the "Instant ON Listing Process." When I go to a house and meet the sellers, the entire marketing system takes one hour from the time I arrive until they are *"live"* on the MLS with all room sizes, all photos, and getting showings right away. I get a lot more listings with that system in place than in my early days, when I had no systems and was "winging it" at appointments.

I mentioned earlier that it shouldn't take 120 hours to close two transactions. Per national statistics, the average real estate agent closes four to six transactions per year. If a typical, full-time agent works twenty hours per week for fifty weeks, they would work 1,000 hours in a year. At the national average of six sales per year, that means they spent 166 hours per transaction. The average full-time real estate agent probably closes more like twelve to twenty-four properties per year. But whether they close one or ten per month, many agents and their team members fall into a trap, believing some transactions take longer than others and that the unpredictable can't be controlled. An agent working mainly with buyers might think they can't control the number of houses a buyer will look at or how long a listing appointment will take. The reality is, with the right system, you can.

I thought I had no control over my time early in my career. But as the years went by, I understood what Michael was saying when he explained estimating. So I spent years tracking everything I did in real estate transactions. I looked for ways to streamline everything. How to manage every aspect of the real estate business. I took all the great ideas from other agents around the globe and refined our systems until we created the ones I use today to control time and get more done. To this day I know I can go on five listing appointments per day, five days a week, and the system will crank smoothly. That is twenty-five listings per week, one hundred listings per month, 1,200 listings per year. This is how the new age of real estate is beginning to create agent teams and businesses that are closing over 1,000 transactions per year. But only a few agents and teams are willing to do what it takes to get there. Yet everyone has the same opportunity to create an "E-Myth" real estate business.

Here is another number to help you understand why estimating is critical. In the "People" chapter, we explained that the average person moves every five to ten years, and if you add five people to your database every day, that would add 1,200 people to your pipeline each year. If you did this for five years, you would have 6,000 people in your database. That means 600 to 1,200 people in your database would be moving every year. That number does not include sign calls, internet leads, ad calls, open house leads, or referrals from clients. That is just business from the people you added to your database over that five-year period. Is there a chance you will be selling real estate in the next ten years? Then double the number. That is over 2,400 people moving every year. *Every year.*

Real estate is a stressful process for every person involved in the transaction. Starting with you, the agent, the client, and everyone else involved—including the inspector, lender, title company, warranty company, contractors, roofers, plumbers, and every employee who works with all these people. What if working with you meant that every person you cross paths with had an incredible experience and loved going through the process every single time they worked with you? What if they could say, "I absolutely *love* working with this agent. Their transactions are always smooth, and they have got it figured out!" Let me ask, would more agents want to see your listings? Would more vendors want to be working with you and refer anyone they know to you?

Estimating doesn't stop with just what you do. If you are going to create a Disney-like experience for everyone you meet, you will want to estimate everyone's job throughout the entire process. Including the parts of the process you don't have control over. Believe me: you can keep more control of the entire process all the way through when you create a system for every little detail.

If you are a single agent just starting out or closing one to two transactions per month, understand that you will be able to test your systems better and tweak them when you get to two to four closings per month. Once you have doubled what you do now and also doubled the results of everyone on the team, you will be able to see more clearly whether they are relying on the system you created. With this book, you can start the process of putting your systems into place.

Look at your current business. If you were closing three properties every day of the month, what would your life look like? Would it be total chaos? What if you created processes to eliminate most of the bumps in a transaction? Would you be able to close more deals? If you don't create the systems, you won't know how many more deals you can close.

When you build checkpoints into your system, trust your system to do the heavy work, and plug all the holes in the process, you will experience what it is like to control the transaction every time. You will now have created a McDonald's-like system for your business. The perfect test will be when you help the difficult clients who aren't satisfied with anything you do. I love to put those clients through my systems. My goal is to make them, at least, complacent with the entire experience. I am not saying you will forever eliminate dissatisfied clients. However, you will have more satisfied clients. I personally love taking on the clients other agents consider too demanding. You know who I am talking about. They're the "energy vampires." The clients who are never happy. The ones who call every day after every showing or who want you to take them through every house that hits the market, even though they may never buy a house.

Those types of clients, even when run through your system, will never be your happiest clients. However, if you can get them through your system with little or no stress to yourself, and they come out on the other end with a property, you did your job and what the system was designed to do. Imagine how much business you would have from all the other real estate agents in your community if their client was about to fire them, and they knew you had a system that could get that client to closing. If they knew you as the agent who pays more in referral fees than they make selling houses themselves, your competitors would send you business. Several competitors in the real estate industry call me to be their real estate agent. I consider myself the "Real Estate Agent's Real Estate Agent," and I have a follow-up system that keeps me in front of them to remind them I am the one they can count on to get things done.

You can see how important it is to dial in to every detail that makes you so awesome. Document everything you do and the time it takes to do it. More importantly, systematize it so you aren't the one trying to do one hundred sales per year, or the 857 sales per year every one of us has the potential to do just by focusing on adding five people to your database each day for the next five years. The purpose here is to build something scalable so it can be salable. When you build your real estate business with the intention to sell it someday (whether you do or not), you will realize that the business doesn't have to control your life. This new business model is designed to fund your life.

Now let's see what revelations Michael has in store for us as he discusses the subject of *clients*. ❧

On the Subject
of Clients

Michael E. Gerber

Whether individuals or organizations, we follow those who lead not because we have to, but because we want to. We follow those who lead not for them, but for ourselves.

—Simon Sinek

When it comes to the business of real estate, the best definition of clients I've ever heard is this:

Clients: *very special people who drive most real estate agents crazy.*

Does that work for you?

After all, it's a rare client who shows any appreciation for what a real estate agent has to go through to do the job as promised. Don't they always think the price is too high? And don't they focus on problems, broken promises, and the mistakes they think you make, rather than all the ways you bend over backward to give them what they need?

Do you ever hear other real estate agents voice these complaints? More to the point, have you ever voiced them yourself? Well, you're not alone. I have yet to meet a real estate agent who doesn't suffer from a strong case of client confusion.

Client confusion is about:

- What your client really wants
- How to communicate effectively with your client
- How to keep your client happy
- How to deal with client dissatisfaction
- Whom to call a client

Confusion 1: What Your Client Really Wants

Your clients aren't just people; they're very specific kinds of people. Let me share with you the six categories of clients as seen from the E-Myth marketing perspective: (1) tactile clients, (2) neutral clients, (3) withdrawal clients, (4) experimental clients, (5) transitional clients, and (6) traditional clients.

Your entire marketing strategy must be based on which type of client you are dealing with. Each of the six client types spends money on real estate services for very different, and identifiable, reasons. These are:

- Tactile clients get their major gratification from interacting with other people.
- Neutral clients get their major gratification from interacting with inanimate objects (computers, cars, information).
- Withdrawal clients get their major gratification from interacting with ideas (thoughts, concepts, stories).
- Experimental clients rationalize their buying decisions by perceiving that what they bought is new, revolutionary, and innovative.
- Transitional clients rationalize their buying decisions by perceiving that what they bought is dependable and reliable.
- Traditional clients rationalize their buying decisions by perceiving that what they bought is cost-effective, a good deal, and worth the money.

In short:

- If your client is tactile, you have to emphasize the *people* of your business.
- If your client is neutral, you have to emphasize the *technology* of your business.
- If your client is a withdrawal client, you have to emphasize the *idea* of your business.
- If your client is experimental, you have to emphasize the *uniqueness* of your business.
- If your client is transitional, you have to emphasize the *dependability* of your business.
- If your client is traditional, you have to talk about the *financial competitiveness* of your business.

What your clients want is determined by who they are. Who they are is regularly demonstrated by what they do. Think about the clients with whom you do business. Ask yourself: In which of the categories would I place them? What do they do for a living?

If your client is a mechanical engineer, for example, it's probably safe to assume he's a neutral client. If another one of your clients is a cardiologist, she's probably tactile. Accountants tend to be traditional, and software engineers are often experimental.

Having an idea about which categories your clients may fall into is helpful to figuring out what they want. Of course, there's no exact science to it, and human beings constantly defy stereotypes. So don't take my word for it. You'll want to make your own analysis of the clients you serve.

Confusion 2: How to Communicate Effectively with Your Client

The next step in the client satisfaction process is to decide how to magnify the characteristics of your company most likely to appeal to your preferred category of client. That begins with what marketing people call your *positioning strategy*.

What do I mean by *positioning* your company? You position your company with words. A few well-chosen words that tell your clients exactly what they want to hear. In marketing lingo, those words are called your USP, or unique selling proposition.

For example, if you are targeting tactile clients (ones who love people), your USP could be: "Value Real Estate, where the feelings of people *really* count!"

If you are targeting experimental clients (ones who love new, revolutionary things), your USP could be: "Value Real Estate, where living on the edge is a way of life!" In other words, when they choose to schedule an appointment with you, they can count on both your services and techniques to be on the cutting edge of the real estate industry.

Is this starting to make sense? Do you see how the ordinary things most real estate agents do to get clients can be done in a significantly more effective way?

Once you understand the essential principles of marketing the E-Myth way, the strategies by which you attract clients can make an enormous difference in your market share.

Confusion 3: How to Keep Your Client Happy

Let's say you've overcome the first two confusions. Great. Now how do you keep your client happy?

Very simple . . . just keep your promise! And make sure your client knows you kept your promise every step of the way.

In short, giving your clients what they think they want is the key to keeping your clients (or anyone else, for that matter) really happy.

If your clients need to interact with people (high touch, tactile), make certain they do.

If they need to interact with things (high-tech, neutral), make certain they do.

If they need to interact with ideas (in their head, withdrawal), make certain they do.

And so forth.

At E-Myth, we call this your *client fulfillment system*. It's the step-by-step process by which you do the task you've contracted to do and deliver what you've promised—on time, every time.

But what happens when your clients are not happy? What happens when you've done everything I've mentioned here and your client is still dissatisfied?

Confusion 4: How to Deal with Client Dissatisfaction

If you have followed each step up to this point, client dissatisfaction will be rare. But it will still occur—people are people, and some people will always be dissatisfied with something. Here's what to do about it:

- Always listen to what your clients are saying. And never interrupt while they're saying it.

- After you're sure you've heard all of your client's complaint, make absolutely certain you understand what she said by posing a question, such as: "Can I repeat what you've just told me, Ms. Harton, to make absolutely certain I understand you?"

- Secure your client's acknowledgment that you have heard her complaint accurately.

- Apologize for whatever your client thinks you did that dissatisfied her, even if you didn't do it!

- After your client has acknowledged your apology, ask her exactly what would make her happy.

- Repeat what your client told you would make her happy, and get her acknowledgment that you have heard correctly.

- If at all possible, give your client exactly what she has asked for.

You may be thinking, "But what if my client wants something totally impossible?" Don't worry. If you've followed my recommendations to the letter, what your client asks for will seldom seem unreasonable.

Confusion 5: Whom to Call a Client

At this stage, it's important to ask yourself some questions about the kind of clients you hope to attract to your company:

- Which types of clients would you most like to do business with?
- Where do you see your real market opportunities?
- Whom would you like to work with, provide services to, and position your business for?

In short, *it's all up to you*. No mystery. No magic. Just a systematic process for shaping your company's future. But you must have the passion to pursue the process. And you must be absolutely clear about every aspect of it . . .

- Until you know your clients as well as you know yourself
- Until all your complaints about clients are a thing of the past
- Until you accept the undeniable fact that client acquisition and client satisfaction are more science than art

But unless you're willing to grow your company, you'd better not follow any of these recommendations. Because if you do what I'm suggesting, it's going to grow.

This brings us to the subject of *growth*. But first, let's read what Brad has to say about *marketing*. ❧

CHAPTER

16

Everyone You Meet Will Be Moving

Brad Korn

Building a World Class Company is a commitment to the integration of passion, purpose, and practice.
—Michael E. Gerber, *E-Myth Mastery: The Seven Essential Disciplines for Building a World Class Company*

Remember, everybody moves at some point. That means every person you meet from today forward is a potential client over the next five to ten years. You want a lead conversion system that will convert every one of those people into a buyer, seller, or investor sometime over the next five or ten years. Is every contact record in your database on a five- to ten-year conversion plan that keeps you in front of them consistently and persistently? Are you or a team member talking to every person you ever meet, on purpose, every year throughout the year?

If the answer is no, don't despair! The entire industry continues to sell us conversion systems that are as hands-off as possible and

135

will keep us all in the 1 percent to 3 percent conversion game forever. What most real estate agents miss is the 97 percent to 99 percent of people who aren't moving *right now*. One percent to 2 percent of everyone you meet is in the process of moving every month. You have to talk to all of them to ensure you are in front of the right 1 percent to 2 percent each month. This doesn't mean you have to talk to everyone every month. It is not physically possible for one person to talk to 6,000 people every month. It is not duplicable, either. It is about a consistent touch over time. Agents who keep in touch with their database through a relationship-based drip plan can grow their business six to eight times faster and not work as hard as an agent following traditional lead generation methods— which means trying to persuade strangers to do business with them.

The reason conversion rates are so low is because of the real estate math. If the average person moves every five years, that means 80 percent of the people you are cold calling every month are not moving this year. Why pound them with real estate drip stuff? You don't have to. They aren't moving yet. Most agents don't even put those 80 percent in their system. But the reality is that each one of those 80 percent is moving—just not this year. They don't know when they are moving, and we don't know which 20 percent are moving. What we know for sure is that they will be moving sometime in the next five to ten years. You can't ignore the 80 percent. You just need a better, non-real estate way to stay in touch with them until they become the 20 percent who are ready to move. If you don't add them to the database or stay in front of them regularly, you won't be in front of them next year or ten years from now when they are ready to buy or sell. The odds they will remember you five years from now are slim.

When you apply *The E-Myth Real Estate Agent* to your real estate business, you protect yourself from failure. Our industry is at a turning point. Real estate has gotten a bad reputation. We are ranked in some studies as an untrustworthy industry. Consumers are realizing they don't need an agent to put a sign in the yard. Sometimes they just pay a flat fee to have their property posted on MLS and call it done. Anyone who has been in the real estate business for a while knows the MLS doesn't make the property sell. If it did, there would be no expired listings. If MLS were the answer, everyone would just use the agent with the cheapest commission. The reality is, there is much more to selling a home than just putting it on MLS.

Against all odds, real estate can be what you hoped it would be when you went to real estate school. You have access to everything you need to deliver quality service to your clients and get them the best results no matter the market conditions. It is your obligation to yourself and your family and colleagues to raise the bar in the real estate industry if you want to make this your career and fund your awesome life. This is one of the last career options where an average Joe has the potential to make unlimited income.

There is some confusion as to who our customer really is. The answer is surprisingly simple: every person on the planet is your customer. That's true even if you don't end up helping everyone buy or sell a home right now, today. A unique perk in the real estate industry is referrals. If your real estate license is current, you can get paid for referring buyers and sellers to another real estate agent. No matter where they move, if you have a real estate license, you can receive a referral commission for connecting that lead with another agent in another state or country.

Of course, you can also receive referrals from the people in your own database if they know someone who needs the services of a real estate agent. Therefore, literally every person you meet and know anywhere in the world is a potential source of income for your real estate business.

You really can't help everyone on the planet yet. You need to develop a focus and direction as you create your new company (or new way of doing business). Define your perfect client and build your systems to service that client. If you have a buyer or seller lead who doesn't fit your perfect client profile, you can refer them to another agent and be compensated when that transaction closes. Did you know less than 5 percent of all relocations pay a referral fee to another agent? That means 95 percent of all people who move—people we may have talked to once in our lifetime—did not come back to us to ensure they were referred to another great agent who could have helped them, which could have gotten us a referral commission. Therefore, the experience they had was determined by whatever random real estate agent they found in their market. Think about how many people move out of the area without being referred. That is a huge amount of lost income in referral fees.

What Your Client Really Wants

When you create the perfect system, you can take your business to the next level and automate it with the ability to service each type of client personality. That's true whether it's the client who wants to hear from you, personally, multiple times a day or the client who says, "Leave me alone until it's sold." When you have systems, you can service both clients with the system that suits them best. Do you have a system in place to tell you whether your client wants to communicate primarily by text or wants to see you regularly, face-to-face? If you don't, their expectation and their experience may not be what you want them to experience. I hope you can see how not implementing a well-oiled system could make your business as unpredictable as a roller-coaster ride—not just for you, but for your client as well.

I have studied and internalized different personality types and understand the value of knowing how people think, what they want and expect. I have tweaked my perfect client fulfillment system to deliver the experience that matches their personality without causing extra work for me or anyone working with me. The turnkey systems I use to service all types of people keep me focused on ensuring they have a great experience. I don't change my entire system for everyone, other than in the way I communicate during the process.

If you have 99 things to do from the time you list a house until it is sold, you can use the same system for the person who wants personal contact and the person who doesn't. By creating your perfect process and getting every step of your system in that process, you can duplicate that process for different personalities by adding special steps. The result? An even-better-than-McDonald's system. What you have done is completely systematized and automated the "custom order" process.

Here's how the system works. You might apply more calls and personal touches to the plan when you have a tactile client. Creating checkpoints in the system will ensure everything stays on track and that your client has the experience you and your team want to deliver. The system can be set up to encourage clients to meet at your office if they want to see you face-to-face. If you have a techy client, your system can give them web links to everything about their property or the property they want to buy. And most importantly, each process will help you get the ultimate result—an incredible experience that achieved the client's goal with the least inconvenience.

A more advanced system would be able to merge these systems if, for example, you have a married couple where one is hands-off and the other spouse wants personal, one-on-one attention. Too many times agents serve one spouse without realizing the other spouse is the true decision maker and is experiencing the worst real estate transaction of their life. They are the ones talking with their co-workers and friends, spreading the word about how horrible the entire experience with you is. Have you ever thought your communication with one client was going great only to find out you were being fired by the other spouse so they could try their friend's real estate agent? Surveying everyone involved throughout the transaction and getting honest feedback can help you create the foolproof, predictable systems that allow you to deliver a high level of service for every client you work with.

How to Communicate with Your Clients Effectively

The major complaint from consumers in our industry stems from a lack of communication throughout the process. A lot of things happen in a real estate transaction, and a lot of people are involved to complete that sale from beginning to end. This is one of the largest purchases people make in their life, and no matter how well you keep in touch with them, someone always feels like he or she didn't know what was going to happen next.

When your systems and processes are perfected and automated to reach clients how and when they want to be reached, you will see your business explode. A word of caution, though. If your process isn't systematized and automated, you could get stuck being an E-Myth Technician the rest of your career. You will only be able to help a certain number of people by yourself. If you don't have a system that allows every team member—whether it is one or 1,000 people—to do the same thing you do, then hundreds, if not thousands, of potential clients will be left to take their chances with an agent who may not have read this book or does not run his or her business like a business. That really isn't fair to those consumers. Everyone should have the opportunity to have an incredible experience when buying, selling or investing in real estate. Shouldn't the entire transaction be fun, as well as organized, and close on time?

Part of your communications is getting people to do business with you. This is a huge challenge when you are starting out. The consumer may think all real estate agents are alike, so why not use the cheapest one? Most agents will join their local and national boards and have access to the MLS, so why should they choose you over their brother or sister who is also a real estate agent? Once you figure out the secret sauce that makes people choose you and your systems to give them an experience worth talking about, you will win them over and get more referrals. You want them to feel like they are your only client. A system gives consumers the confidence they hired the right person. The system keeps them informed throughout the transaction, so they know what happens next. Consumers want to feel like they are working with someone who cares about this move as much as they do and listens to them. They don't really care how many people you have helped or how busy you are right now. They want you to treat them like their transaction is the most important thing, and the only thing, you have going on right now.

If you pay attention to what successful agents share, you can shortcut the process to finding perfect systems. That's what I did. I tracked my results. When I heard a script and used it, but didn't get the results I wanted, I would change a word here or there until I got the result I wanted every time. For example, at your listing appointment, a seller might say, "We don't really have to sell" and "We don't want to give it away." They have you there to help them sell their house. What do they mean they don't have to sell? Your scripts and wording need to communicate that they are selling because they want to, and they are not giving it away. When you perfect your wording to communicate to the client that what they need to hear is the same thing they want to hear, then you have a predictable result system.

I didn't want to have 50 percent of my listings expire. If the seller was not motived, I would not list that home for sale. My mind-set was, if I am at someone's kitchen table talking to them about selling their home, then I am going to get that listing and get them to price it right. Once I got their property listed, I was going to deliver an experience that had them saying, *"Wow,* thank you so much for all your hard work. You did an incredible job." I just kept working and working on my systems until I got predictable results every time. I did not want to take a stab at it and see what happened. If I operated that way, I would have to go back to the grindstone every day to find the next deal. I wanted my systems to ensure that I got my client the most equity possible for current market conditions.

How to Keep Your Clients Happy

Every client is different. While you are documenting and creating your client fulfillment system, you will realize just how many of your clients are not having an incredible experience. You may see holes in your current way of doing business that many of your clients are slipping through—and most of them won't tell you they are disappointed. They start to lose trust, faith, and confidence that you and/or your team are the right ones to help them. When you have an automated system in place, you can plug those holes forever and move toward that Disney experience. You can control that experience and make it predictable for everyone you do business with.

The key to creating this new, better business model using *The E-Myth Real Estate Agent* success systems starts with the client fulfillment system. When you go through the perfect process and automate that process, you and anyone you work with will know how everyone on the team is connected to each client and their experience. When you review your processes every year and continually improve on the experience, you will begin to have more and more happy clients. This is the heart of your clients being completely satisfied throughout the entire process. Have a system for your system to document what everyone does and go through every step of your process as a team to build the perfect process. That is how you will get buy-in from everyone on the team and in your business.

A view of the perfect processes

Close-up of the action items

How to Deal with Client Dissatisfaction

As you start this journey to become an E-Myth real estate agent you are going to get frustrated and see things about your business and your clients you have not seen before. As I went through this process, I realized that even though we were systematizing this great experience for our clients, we had a negative force pushing back on the other side: the other agents involved. Sometimes it was even the inspectors, or lenders, or just about anyone in the transaction who didn't have a similar system or hadn't read *The E-Myth*.

If everyone isn't running a perfect system in their business and are not doing their job as well as you think they should, your system needs to pick up the slack. I learned that when bad things happen in a transaction and someone in the process doesn't do their job, the transaction can get messy fast. That can cause a delay in closing or, worse yet, kill the contract. The client will most likely look to the real estate agent and hold our team responsible even if we did everything right.

An automated system allows you to be in the moment at every moment and not be consumed with finding the next deal before this one is finished. It allows you to hold others accountable, and to know when and where you need to tweak the system.

The perfect system means you don't have to worry about firing employees! The system will choke them out if they don't use it. Your system should be perfected to the point that if your people use the system, it will deliver an incredible experience for the client and everyone involved. Systems allow you to do what you do best: solve problems. You can get out of "reactive mode" so you can listen and devise a solution that will get everyone back to their happy zone.

Remember, you are going to be creating the ultimate real estate experience. Each client from this day forward will help you document where and when to tweak your current system until you perfect it. The unhappy clients, for right now, will be the best clients you have and will contribute to creating the perfect real estate transaction.

Whom to Call a Client

As I mentioned before, in real estate, everyone is technically a client. Create your perfect process around your perfect client.

If you add one hundred people to your database every month for the next ten years, you will have over 12,000 people in your capture system. When you get to that point, you will have the luxury of working with your perfect client more often. Think about what the referral income would look like on a business that generated 1,200-plus sales opportunities per year, you only worked with the people you wanted to, and you referred everyone else to another agent. You will have created a real estate empire, and you won't be physically working with any clients because you are running an E-Myth real estate agent business.

Michael has explained that until you define who your client is, eliminate every complaint, and create the ultimate experience for every one of your clients, you are in the system perfection zone. Determine what causes stress for you, your clients, or anyone involved in the transaction, and create a system for eliminating all that stress. That will create your perfect client fulfillment system.

Now let's consider Michael's thoughts about *growth*. ❖

CHAPTER 17

On the Subject
of Growth

Michael E. Gerber

The problem in my life and other people's lives is not the absence of knowing what to do, but the absence of doing it.

—Peter F. Drucker

The rule of business growth says that every business, like every child, is destined to grow. Needs to grow. Is determined to grow.

Once you've created your real estate business, once you've shaped the idea of it, the most natural thing for it to do is to . . . grow! And if you stop it from growing, it will die.

Once a real estate agent has started a company, it's his or her job to help it grow. To nurture it and support it in every way. To infuse it with

- Purpose
- Passion

145

- Will
- Belief
- Personality
- Method

As your company grows, it naturally changes. And as it changes from a small company to something much bigger, you will begin to feel out of control. News flash: that's because you are out of control.

Your company has exceeded your know-how, sprinted right past you, and now it's taunting you to keep up. That leaves you two choices: grow as big as your company demands you grow, or try to hold your company at its present level—at the level you feel most comfortable.

The sad fact is that most real estate agents do the latter. They try to keep their company small, securely within their comfort zone. Doing what they know how to do, what they feel most comfortable doing. It's called playing it safe.

But as the company grows, the number, scale, and complexity of tasks will grow, too, until they threaten to overwhelm the real estate agent. More people are needed. More space. More money. Everything seems to be happening at the same time. A hundred balls are in the air at once.

As I've said throughout this book: most real estate agents are not entrepreneurs. They aren't true businesspeople at all, but technicians suffering from an entrepreneurial seizure. Their philosophy of coping with the workload can be summarized as "just do it," rather than figure out how to get it done through other people using innovative systems to produce consistent results.

Given most real estate agents' inclination to be the master juggler in their company, it's not surprising that as complexity increases, as work expands beyond their ability to do it, as money becomes more elusive, they are just holding on, desperately juggling more and more balls. In the end, most collapse under the strain.

You can't expect your company to stand still. You can't expect your company to stay small. A company that stays small and depends on you to do everything isn't a company—it's a job!

Yes, just like your children, your business must be allowed to grow, to flourish, to change, to become more than it is. In this way, it will match your vision. And you know all about vision, right? You'd better. It's what you do best!

Do you feel the excitement? You should. After all, you know what your company is but not what it can be.

It's either going to grow or die. The choice is yours, but it is a choice that must be made. If you sit back and wait for change to overtake you, you will always have to answer no to this question: are you ready?

This brings us to the subject of *change*. But first, let's see what Brad has to say about *growth*. ✤

CHAPTER 18

Change Your Focus and Get 4 to 5 Times More Business

Brad Korn

*The typical small business owner is only 10 percent Entrepreneur,
20 percent Manager, and 70 percent Technician.*
—Michael E. Gerber, *The E-Myth Revisited: Why Most
Small Businesses Don't Work and What to Do About It*

One of the most profound statements from my early days in business is from Michael Gerber's *The E-Myth Revisited*. In it, he says, "If your business isn't growing, it's dying." I have been fortunate to hear the right messages at the right times and learn from the best people in the industry. Most important, I implemented the things I learned. Everything I learned and implemented helped to grow my business every day.

In this chapter, we are talking about growth. Keep an open mind and understand the message I am sharing with you. The phrase, "If your business isn't growing, it's dying" is one of the most enlightening messages you can get from this book. Suspend any thoughts you have about what you think growth is. Growth is not a 5 percent or 10 percent increase in business. Growth is not one great year and then a so-so year the next year. Growth is growing your business exponentially, increasing profits dramatically, and leveraging systems so, instead of working harder, you work less as you grow. So many agents get stuck in the Technician role their entire life because they do not want to "manage" a bunch of people. But growth is not about people. It is about creating a franchise-like business that is scalable, so it could be saleable if you choose.

Let's start at the core of growth for your real estate business. Growth is not some automated lead generation machine that is going to send you leads every day. You know by now that only 1 percent to 3 percent of all cold (or even somewhat warm) leads will turn into business. You also know that every person you meet is likely to buy or sell a house in the next five to ten years.

The 1 percent to 3 percent of people moving right now are what I call "fall out of the sky" business. If the average person moves every five years, then 20 percent of the population is moving each year. However, only one of the next ten people moving this year is moving right now, this month.

100 People	1,000 People
Every 5 Years	Every 5 Years
20 People	200 People
20 over 12 months	200 over 12 months
1.5+ per month	**16+ per month**

You can grow your business simply by thinking of every person you meet from this day forward as potential business. You already put effort into getting into conversation with them. Now think of every conversation as your future pipeline business and put them into your lead conversion system. You will pack your pipeline of business to double or triple your current business. In fact, you can grow your business six to eight times by applying a personal touch system to your business. This could be your opportunity to get off the "lead generation" grindstone forever.

If you have your real estate license, you are probably well into your life and career. Time is clicking away every day. Don't wait any longer. Today is the day to build a successful real estate business.

Are you looking forward to working day in and day out, every day until the day you leave this earth? I advise you to "stop and smell the roses." You will begin to realize just what that cliché means when you can enjoy life more. You don't have to miss any of it because you were told you must work hard.

I was fortunate to figure this all out when I was thirty years old. I systematized my lead generation, lead conversion, and my client fulfillment back-end transaction management so I could make sure my business was running while I was at my daughters' sporting events, plays, singing programs, parents' day at school, etc. Those systems gave me time to be by my wife Sonya's side every day for five months while she was in a coma. During that time business went on as usual with my two team members selling almost one hundred properties that year. Thank goodness my success wasn't tied to me being on the phone every day generating new business.

Today's real estate agent continually hears the phrase "lead generation." Lead generation is what drives a business, yet if you talk to most agents, they cringe when they hear the word. I know why. Because after putting systems in place that generate an easy one hundred sales a year from my database, I still do not like getting on the phone with strangers to persuade them to do business with me.

Can I do it? Heck, yes! I can convert with the best of them. However, as a daily routine, it is not fun. If it were, every agent in the industry would be in their office every day for four to six hours dialing numbers. I have not seen that in any real estate office, ever. Sure, I see agents do it for a day, but they won't do it naturally, and they won't do it day after day after day. Even when they do commit to dialing for hours, very few agents put everything—names, addresses, phone numbers and emails—into their database. They just call for the next potential buyer or seller, and forget the rest.

If you had a good conversation, but the people said they were not moving right now, you should still put them in your follow-up plan. They are going to move one day, and you just had a good conversation with them. Just don't blast them with your automated real estate drip plan.

When you master the skill to get all their contact information, you can stay in front of them several different ways. Whatever information is missing will limit the marketing medium you use to convert them into closed business when they do decide to move. If you have email leads dumping into your database automatically, then pay attention to what I am saying. This next statement could explain why your business isn't doubling or tripling every year and why you feel you are constantly having to "feed the beast" to keep your business going, let alone growing.

Email addresses alone are never going to get you much better than a 1 percent to 3 percent conversion rate. There is no magic subject line or message that will get everyone to do business with you. The conversion happens when you connect with them. Once you connect and have a good conversation and obtain their contact information, you will want to mix the mediums on your follow-up and include more personal touches to stay in front of them.

The E-Myth real estate agent system I created helped me double my business. Once I started using the system, I went from zero sales in year one to $1 million in the second year to $2 million in the third year, $4 million in the fourth year, and $8 million in the fifth year. And I continued to grow my business by sticking to the system. That growth is possible for every real estate agent if you are willing to do what it takes to connect with your leads and implement a systematic follow-up process. Your success and growth will not be reliant on the grindstone of lead generation methods that require you to talk to strangers. I am not saying it is bad to talk to for-sale-by-owners or expired listings, go to a mall, or go door-to-door soliciting. But don't rely on those tactics as your sole method for growth—unless you love doing that kind of thing.

When you create a system that gets you in front of prospects more often, and then stay in front of them, you will increase your chances to convert them into more closed business than if you take the gunshot approach. Review the real estate math:

5 people per day x 5 days a week	=	25 people per week
25 people per week x 4 weeks	=	100 people per month
100 people per month x 12 months a year	=	1,200 people per year
1,200 people added to your database over the next 5 years	=	6,000 connected contact records

Every real estate agent needs to hear this message, whether just starting out or having been in business for years! You can start your E-Myth real estate agent growth plan today. I call it the Make the Phone Ring Again (MTPRA) plan, because when you connect, capture, and then apply your automated conversion plan, you will get more business by being the only real estate agent who stays in touch until your prospects are ready to move. It is the ultimate top-of-mind awareness marketing plan.

What are the numbers you can expect? Over the next five years the 1,200 people you added the first year will have all moved. That is 1,200 opportunities over the next five years, or 240 sales every year for the next five years! If you only get half of this right and only get the systems partially created, you could have 120 sales every year. Let's say you really mess it up and only get it 25 percent right, and all you do is add five people a day and write a note to everyone you meet, then forget to stay in touch. Twenty-five percent of the system in place could still get you sixty sales a year, every year, without having to talk to strangers or cold call for business. In fact, when you focus on this for the next five years and add 6,000 good connections and relationships to your database, you have the opportunity for 600 to 1,200 contacts who will be buying real estate *every year!* If you did a great job of keeping in touch with them and are the first one they think of, you won't have to compete for their business.

Following the Five-a-Day Plan will grow your real estate business naturally and at a pace you can manage. Your systems will be like having an assistant and will streamline all your processes, so you can focus on more dollar-productive activities, like adding more people to your database and making follow-up calls. You can use your systems as leverage to bank three to four months of extra cash to cover the salaries of the people you might hire as you get busier. The "build it and the business will come" business model can put real estate agents out of business by burying them in debt. That stress to pay the bills every month can keep them from ever growing to a point where they can get out of the day-to-day activities. They get trapped doing it, doing it, doing it every day, and then real estate controls their life. A commercial that ran years ago showed agents working while their clients were enjoying life, and the tag line was "Real estate is my life." Yes, we sell lifestyle to our real estate clients, but no one said you must sacrifice your life to give your clients perfection.

Where do you start? It comes back to your original dream, mission, vision, and purpose for getting into real estate. Was it for you to have a better life because of the income potential? Was it because you had a horrible real estate transaction and thought, "I could provide better service than that," or was it because you wanted a business with flexibility in your schedule? No matter the reason, when you figure out your why and have the will to make it happen, all you must do is apply the E-Myth principles through the already proven E-Myth real estate agent systems, and you can get excited about real estate and be even more excited about growing your business to gain the lifestyle you want.

Remember, growth doesn't mean you have to work harder or do more stressful deals. In fact, with the right systems, you will feel as though it takes very little effort to help one hundred to 150 real estate clients have an incredible experience without some monster-sized team supporting it all. You can do that with just a few people. Once you get to that point in your business, you will see the potential for growth and how your real estate business could give five times as many people the opportunity for a great real estate experience.

If you were hoping for a chapter on "Growth" that included how to hire employees and team members who will convert leads better and sell more houses, refer to Chapter 9, "On the Subject of People." Just adding people is not a guaranteed growth method. This chapter covers a plan for guaranteed growth through systems that people run. This method requires you get the three-legged automated systems (lead capture, lead conversion and client fulfillment systems) in place before you build a real estate business.

Once you do that, you are ready to grow with people. Your systems will have been perfected enough to help your future hires deliver an extraordinary level of service for your clients, customers, co-workers, team, and everyone else involved in every part of your real estate transaction.

On that note, let's see in the next chapter what Michael has to say about *change*. ❧

On the Subject
of Change

Michael E. Gerber

Our Leaders of today need the philosophy of the past, paired with the
scientific knowledge and technology of tomorrow.

—Anders Indset

S o your company is growing. That means, of course, that it's also
changing. Which means it's driving you and everyone in your
life crazy.

That's because, to most people, change is a diabolical thing. Tell
most people they've got to change, and their first instinct is to crawl
into a hole. Nothing threatens their existence more than change.
Nothing cements their resistance more than change. Nothing.

Yet for the past forty years, that's exactly what I've been proposing
to small business owners: the need to change. Not for the sake of
change itself, but for the sake of their lives.

I've talked to countless real estate agents whose hopes weren't
being realized through their company; whose lives were consumed

by work; who slaved increasingly longer hours for decreasing pay; whose dissatisfaction grew as their enjoyment shriveled. Real estate agents whose company had become the worst job in the world; whose money was out of control; whose employees were a source of never-ending hassles, just like their clients, their bank, and, increasingly, even their families.

More and more, these real estate agents spent their time alone, dreading the unknown and anxious about the future. And even when they were with people, they didn't know how to relax. Their mind was always on the job. They were distracted by work, by the thought of work. By the fear of falling behind.

And yet, when confronted with their condition and offered an alternative, most of the same real estate agents strenuously resisted. They assumed that if there were a better way of doing business, they already would have figured it out. They derived comfort from knowing what they believed they already knew. They accepted the limitations of being a real estate agent; or the truth about people; or the limitations of what they could expect from their clients, their employees, their team members, their bankers—even their family and friends.

In short, most real estate agents I've met over the years would rather live with the frustrations they already have than risk enduring new frustrations.

Isn't that true of most people you know? Rather than opening up to the infinite number of possibilities life offers, they prefer to shut their life down to respectable limits. After all, isn't that the most reasonable way to live?

I think not. I think we must learn to let go. I think that if you fail to embrace change, it will inevitably destroy you.

Conversely, by opening yourself to change, you give your real estate business the opportunity to get the most from your talents.

Let me share with you an original way to think about change, about life, about who we are and what we do. About the stunning notion of expansion and contraction.

Contraction versus Expansion

"Our salvation," a wise man once said, "is to allow." That is, to be open, to let go of our beliefs, to change. Only then can we move from a point of view to a viewing point.

That wise man was Thaddeus Golas, the author of a small, powerful book entitled *The Lazy Man's Guide to Enlightenment* (Seed Center, 1971).

Among the many inspirational things he had to say was this compelling idea:

> The basic function of each being is expanding and contracting. Expanded beings are permeative; contracted beings are dense and impermeative. Therefore each of us, alone or in combination, may appear as space, energy, or mass, depending on the ratio of expansion to contraction chosen, and what kind of vibrations each of us expresses by alternating expansion and contraction. Each being controls his own vibrations.

In other words, Golas tells us that the entire mystery of life can be summed up in two words: *expansion* and *contraction*. He goes on to say:

> We experience expansion as awareness, comprehension, understanding, or whatever we wish to call it.
>
> When we are completely expanded, we have a feeling of total awareness, of being one with all life.
>
> At that level we have no resistance to any vibrations or interactions of other beings. It is timeless bliss, with unlimited choice of consciousness, perception, and feeling.
>
> When a [human] being is totally contracted, he is a mass particle, completely imploded.
>
> To the degree that he is contracted, a being is unable to be in the same space with others, so contraction is felt as fear, pain, unconsciousness, ignorance, hatred, evil, and a whole host of strange feelings.
>
> At an extreme [of contraction, a human being] has the feeling of being completely insane, of resisting everyone and everything, of being unable to choose the content of his consciousness.

*Of course, these are just the feelings appropriate to mass vibra-
tion levels, and he can get out of them at any time by expanding,
by letting go of all resistance to what he thinks, sees, or feels.*

Stay with me here. Because what Golas says is profoundly important. When you're feeling oppressed, overwhelmed, exhausted by
more than you can control—contracted, as Golas puts it—you can
change your state to one of expansion.

According to Golas, the more contracted we are, the more threatened by change; the more expanded we are, the more open to change.

In our most enlightened—that is, open—state, change is as
welcome as non-change. Everything is perceived as a part of ourselves.
There is no inside or outside. Everything is one thing. Our sense of
isolation is transformed to a feeling of ease, of light, of joyful relationship with everything.

As infants, we didn't even think of change in the same way,
because we lived those first days in an unthreatened state. Insensitive
to the threat of loss, most young children are only aware of *what is*.
Change is simply another form of *what is*. Change just *is*.

However, when we are in our most contracted—that is, closed—
state, change is the most extreme threat. If the known is what I have,
then the unknown must be what threatens to take away what I
have. Change, then, is the unknown. And the unknown is fear. It's
like being between trapezes.

- To the fearful, change is threatening because things may
  get worse.
- To the hopeful, change is encouraging because things may
  get better.
- To the confident, change is inspiring because the challenge
  exists to improve things.

If you are fearful, you see difficulties in every opportunity. If you
are fear-free, you see opportunities in every difficulty.

Fear protects what I have from being taken away. But it also
disconnects me from the rest of the world. In other words, fear keeps
me separate and alone.

Here's the exciting part of Golas's message: with this new understanding of contraction and expansion, we can become completely attuned to where we are at all times.

If I am afraid, suspicious, skeptical, and resistant, I am in a contracted state. If I am joyful, open, interested, and willing, I am in an expanded state. Just knowing this puts me on an expanded path. Always remembering this, Golas says, brings enlightenment, which opens me even more.

Such openness gives me the ability to freely access my options. And taking advantage of options is the best part of change. Just as there are infinite ways to greet a client, there are infinite ways to run your company. If you believe Thaddeus Golas, your most exciting option is to be open to all of them.

Because your life is lived on a continuum between the most contracted and most expanded—the most closed and most open— states, change is best understood as the movement from one to the other, and back again.

Most small business owners I've met see change as a thing in itself, as something that just happens to them. Most experience change as a threat. Whenever change shows up at the door, they quickly slam it. Many bolt the door and pile up the furniture. Some even run for their gun.

Few of them understand that change isn't a thing in itself, but rather the manifestation of many things. You might call it the revelation of all possibilities. Think of it as the ability at any moment to sacrifice what we are for what we could become.

Change can either challenge us or threaten us. It's our choice. Our attitude toward change can either pave the way to success or throw up a roadblock.

Change is where opportunity lives. Without change we would stay exactly as we are. The universe would be frozen still. Time would end.

At any given moment, we are somewhere on the path between a contracted and expanded state. Most of us are in the middle of the journey, neither totally closed nor totally open. According to

Golas, change is our movement from one place in the middle toward one of the two ends.

Do you want to move toward contraction or toward enlightenment? Because without change, you are hopelessly stuck with what you've got.

Without change,

- we have no hope;
- we cannot know true joy;
- we will not get better; and
- we will continue to focus exclusively on what we have and the threat of losing it.

All of this negativity contracts us even more, until, at the extreme closed end of the spectrum, we become a black hole so dense that no light can get in or out.

Sadly, the harder we try to hold on to what we've got, the less able we are to do so. So we try still harder, which eventually drags us even deeper into the black hole of contraction.

Are you like that? Do you know anybody who is?

Think of change as the movement between where we are and where we're not. That leaves only two directions for change: either moving forward or slipping backward. We become either more contracted or more expanded.

The next step is to link change to how we feel. If we feel afraid, change is dragging us backward. If we feel open, change is pushing us forward.

Change is not a thing in itself, but a movement of our consciousness. By tuning in, by paying attention, we get clues to the state of our being.

Change, then, is not an outcome or something to be acquired. Change is a shift of our consciousness, of our being, of our humanity, of our attention, of our relationship with all other beings in the universe.

We are either "more in relationship" or "less in relationship." Change is the movement in either of those directions. The exciting part is that *we possess the ability to decide which way we go . . . and to know, in the moment, which way we're moving.*

Closed, open . . . Open, closed. Two directions in the universe. The choice is yours.

Do you see the profound opportunity available to you? What an extraordinary way to live!

Enlightenment is not reserved for the sainted. Rather, it comes to us as we become more sensitive to ourselves. Eventually, we become our own guides, alerting ourselves to our state, moment by moment: *open . . . closed . . . open . . . closed.*

Listen to your inner voice, your ally, and feel what it's like to be open and closed. Experience the instant of choice in both directions.

You will feel the awareness growing. It may be only a flash at first, so be alert. This feeling is accessible, but only if you avoid the black hole of contraction.

Are you afraid that you're totally contracted? Don't be—it's doubtful. The fact that you're still reading this book suggests that you're moving in the opposite direction.

You're more like a running back seeking the open field. You can see the opportunity gleaming in the distance. In the open direction.

Understand that I'm not saying that change itself is a point on the path; rather, it's the all-important movement.

Change is *in you*, not *out there*.

What path are you on? The path of liberation? Or the path of crystallization?

As we know, change can be for the better or for the worse.

If change is happening *inside* of you, it is for the worse only if you remain closed to it. The key, then, is your attitude—your acceptance or rejection of change. Change can be for the better only if you accept it. And it will certainly be for the worse if you don't.

Remember, change is nothing in itself. Without you, change doesn't exist. Change is happening inside of each of us, giving us clues to where we are at any point in time.

Rejoice in change, for it's a sign you are alive.

Are we open? Are we closed? If we're open, good things are bound to happen. If we're closed, things will only get worse.

According to Golas, it's as simple as that. Whatever happens defines where we are. *How* we are is *where* we are. It cannot be any other way.

For change is life.

Charles Darwin wrote, "It is not the strongest of the species that survive, nor the most intelligent, but the one that proves itself most responsive to change."

The growth of your company, then, is its change. Your role is to go with it, to be with it, to share the joy, embrace the opportunities, meet the challenges, learn the lessons.

Remember, there are three kinds of people: (1) those who make things happen, (2) those who let things happen, and (3) those who wonder what the hell happened. The people who make things happen are masters of change. The other two are its victims.

Which type are you?

The Big Change

If all of this is going to mean anything to the life of your company, you have to know when you're going to leave it. At what point, in your company's rise from where it is now to where it can ultimately grow, are you going to sell it? Because if you don't have a clear picture of when you want out, your company is the master of your destiny, not the reverse.

As we stated earlier, the most valuable form of money is equity, and unless your business vision includes your equity and how you will use it to your advantage, you will forever be consumed by your company.

Your company is potentially the best friend you ever had. It is your company's nature to serve you, so let it. If, however, you are not a wise steward, if you do not tell your company what you expect from it, it will run rampant, abuse you, use you, and confuse you.

Change. Growth. Equity.

Focus on the point in the future when you will take leave of your company. Now reconsider your goals in that context. Be specific. Write them down.

Skipping this step is like tiptoeing through earthquake country. Who can say where the fault lies waiting? And who knows exactly when your whole world may come crashing down around you?

Which brings us to the subject of *time*. But first, let's see what Brad has to say about *change*. ✤

CHAPTER 20

Stop Trying to Fix What is Broken

Brad Korn

The key to becoming an entrepreneur is to be willing to start your business all over again.
—Michael E. Gerber, *E-Myth Mastery: The Seven Essential Disciplines for Building a World Class Company*

Routines are comfortable. People do not like change. Sounds reasonable enough, except that people do like change if it makes their life easier and they make more money.

Life isn't always about money, but if you don't make enough money to support your lifestyle, it is hard to argue that it's not important. You can easily obtain a status quo or comfort level in real estate. Anyone selling ten to twenty homes per year can live a comfortable lifestyle. Agents selling forty to fifty homes a year are considered very successful. That keeps a lot of agents stuck at those sales figures for their entire career because it is a comfortable place to be. Stuck may not seem like a bad thing if you are closing forty transactions per year and making $200,000 in commissions. But if you stay in your comfort zone and something in your life pulls you away from your business for a few days, a week, or—in my case—over five months, what would happen to your business? Now, on top of whatever situation you are dealing with, it might be a challenge to pay your bills.

If you continually operate above your comfort zone—which does not take much more effort—you will be sucked back down to "comfort zone" in a crisis, but you can focus your energy where it needs to be. Everyone at every level of success gets into a comfort zone. Without systems, the agent must show up to work every day, or the business will not generate income. If they don't show up for a week or a month, the business would probably have to close. And that means dealing with loss of income.

Everyone has had at least one month in their career where they were concerned about money, so they had to work extra hard, sometimes missing out on pleasurable events. If this is happening to you frequently, it's time for a change.

Change does not have to be drastic. The business model to follow is as simple as doing step one, then step two, then step three—putting your systems in place, and then doing what the system tells you to do. The old saying, "You have to spend money to make money" is wrong. The first step to begin to experience an E-Myth-type real estate business is to meet and connect with five human beings every day, capture their information, and feed them into your database. Once you are feeding the database every day, you'll have to implement step two, systematizing the leads so you stay connected, and then cultivate them over time. That's when step three, a client experience system (also referred to as the client fulfillment system) becomes important. Capturing more leads and converting those leads will begin to get you so much business you will need a system to keep everything running smoothly from contract to closing.

You have to decide to do your business differently than in the past, and until you make that first simple change, the next steps are irrelevant. You must feed your database every day or you will not be able to reap the benefits of this book. If your business isn't growing, it is dying. It might not happen today or tomorrow, but one thing is certain: your business will stay on the roller-coaster ride if you don't implement step one, feeding your database. Adding people to your database should be as natural as brushing your teeth.

When I got into real estate, my first wife had a "real job." We could count on her getting a paycheck every two weeks. That provided insurance for our growing family and, even though the income was never enough for us to live on, it was guaranteed. My real estate income was on an extreme roller-coaster for the first few years, yet I was doing everything I thought I was supposed to be doing. I held open houses three days a week. I knocked on doors. I used the Cole Directory (a reverse telephone directory that had every homeowner's street, name, address and phone number listed) to cold-call neighborhoods. I sent "just listed" and "just sold" cards. Yet I wasn't getting a consistent flow of income. I was not getting rich like I thought I would.

I knew something needed to change after my first three years when I realized those methods don't work as well as I had hoped.

The change, for me, finally came from *The E-Myth Revisited* when I understood that important message from Michael E. Gerber: "If your business isn't growing, it is dying." You must have a systematized place to keep all of your information. A system that reminds you when to contact someone you met months ago.

Once you have a contact management system, feed it every day. Your database or contact management system should have an automated follow-up system that keeps you in front of potential clients consistently. Your system should have personal touches built in to ensure you are top of mind, the first real estate agent they think of, when they decide to buy or sell. The automated emails, mailings, and social media posts are not enough to keep you top of mind with 100 percent of the people you meet. You will be lucky to capture 3 percent of them with a good, fully automated follow-up system without enough personal touches. The personal touch—like a phone call or two-way conversation on social media or text—will get you a much better close rate. The busier you get, the more difficult it will be to keep up with all the personal touches, so you'll want to develop a combination of automated touches plus reminders to make the personal touch. That will get them to call you when they are ready and help you deliver an incredible client/customer experience, so they will want to do business with you again and also refer their friends and family.

Remember, if everyone is going to move, put everyone in your system. That ONE SIMPLE CHANGE made all the difference in the world for me. I started getting consistent results six months after I began feeding five people into my database every day and following up consistently. It was my new ritual, like brushing my teeth. That was when the roller-coaster dips started to flatten out AND pick up speed!

Wherever you are in your real estate business, if you are not getting the results you want and don't have the money or time you want, you have to change the way you are doing business. The great news I have for you is that it's not too late! Just make this one change of adding five people a day to your database, begin implementing *The E-Myth Real Estate Agent* systems, and you can get on a path to double, triple, or quadruple your business. Set up your your lead generation, lead conversion, and client fulfillment systems, and then stick to the system. Every tool or service you are currently using will get better results.

We took a simple interactive voice response (IVR) call/capture system that was getting about 1 percent to 3 percent conversion and increased it to a five-times-better conversion rate just by the way we followed up. We followed up in less than one minute on every lead, AND we called them back three times a day for three days straight. Once we connected with them, we got all their information and turned on the conversion system. That one change boosted our conversion ratio from 3 percent to 15 percent. Once we found out the "three-in-three" system worked, we automated it. Why? Try and keep track of three calls a day for three days straight with a manual system or from memory. Add five people every day to that system and see how long you can keep track. The conversion rates won't be the same if you only make two or three of those nine calls, or if you make those calls one day and then skip a day. The system will keep you on track for predictable results every time.

Today is the day you can make a simple change to amplify the results of everything you do. It is about getting back to the basics. And this time, make it a system that can't be turned off. This is as fundamental and predictable as anything should be. Don't overdo it, and don't overcomplicate the process.

> **It is about getting back to the basics,**
> **and this time,**
> **make it a system that can't be turned off.**

To fully automate as many of the systems mentioned in this book as possible, your contact management provider must be able to accommodate these simple steps:

1) A quick, easy way to feed in five new connections every day without having to log in to your database every time. This is a part of your Lead Generation System.

2) A way for you to review the information going into your database, verify it for accuracy, and assure that the appropriate action plan is started. This is a part of your Management System.

3) An action plan dashboard that tells you what to do next. For example: call a specific contact you have not talked to in four weeks, eight weeks, or three months. The system will notify you when to make your next social media connection. Other "to do's" built into your system will tell you when to write the next note or send a market update. This system could be running with thousands of people at once; however, it will spread the activities out over the year, so you are not doing them in bulk.

A system like this will help you manage thousands of contacts throughout the year versus trying to contact hundreds of people in one day or one week. This shifts you out of the bulk mind-set mentality and into a relationship sort of mind-set. What you are going to do now is start building your New Company alongside your existing business. Don't try to fix what is broken. Your New Company systems will get better results from everything else you currently have running in your business. New Company will improve your Old Company and, over time, replace your Old Company. Real estate can be the vehicle to create and fund the life you really want to have, and that you deserve.

Systems Keep All the Parts Moving

Real estate businesses have lots of moving parts. Big real estate teams rely on lots of people to keep all those parts moving. If you want to see the benefits of systematizing your business, observe what happens when a key member of a big team, or even several people on the team, walk out or quit. The immediate reaction is to hire more people right away. If the company has a people-driven business, then all the new people have to be trained. If they have a system-driven business, and they are continually improving and automating more of their systems, their business will continue as normal. It may not even require the same number of people as before.

My advice to a team going through a turnover would be not to hire anyone until they tweak their systems to be able to handle their business with whoever is still on the team. I'm sure there have been days where a cook at McDonald's walked out without any warning. I'm also sure that if you went to that McDonald's at that time, the burgers would taste the same, and the average consumer coming into that restaurant for lunch would have no idea what was happening behind the scenes. In the same way, I would challenge the agent to get a better system that keeps everything flowing even when your team is expanding or contracting. When you have a system and the system runs your business, it won't matter when people leave you. When people run your business, you are dependent on them for your growth and success forever. People are not predictable; good systems are.

Let's put this last conversation into perspective. If the entire team quits in one day, you might find yourself working sixty or eighty hours that week. The first time this happens, and you don't have the right systems in place, it can be overwhelming. When you have a system-driven business, you can call a temp agency and hire as many people as you need to come run the systems. If the system is fully automated, they won't be required to know anything about real estate to deliver the same level of service you have always delivered. Granted there are many things a licensed real estate agent must do; however, the system should be set up so that anyone could come run your system, and your clients would never know anything was wrong.

If this happens to you, I challenge you not to hire any replacement staff for a month or two until you get all your systems in order and automated to the point where you don't feel overwhelmed. Hiring someone else without your experience or time in the business to come create your systems is not the answer. That will not create an E-Myth-type business guaranteed to deliver extraordinary experiences with average people running the ship. Remember, people just run the system. The system delivers the experience. NOT YOU . . . the system. The system IS you.

This is your chance to make a change from working in reactive mode all the time to creating a predictable business and getting off the income roller-coaster ride. I can promise you this: as you apply *The E-Myth Real Estate Agent* models in your business, they will always be simple. So simple that if you feel like things are getting too complicated and you are feeling lost, you probably made it more complicated than it needs to be. Any E-Myth business is simple to its core. Simple enough anyone can do it. When it is more than that, you have made it more complicated than it needs to be.

The change I am proposing should not feel like change. It is a better way of thinking. It starts with just feeding the database five a day and staying in touch with all those connections on a more predictable, spread-out plan. If you just start with step one, then step two, and then step three, you will look back one day and say, "How did I get here?" You don't need to make drastic changes, and you don't have to have all these systems in place today. You can keep running your old company while creating your new company, a company that is predictable. You have all the information in this book to have all the systems up and running in a short period of time. However, doing it yourself will take time. Be patient. This is the long game. This is building a business that doesn't require you to keep it going day after day.

An early thing you can change is to capitalize on the database you currently have. The reconnect plan is four simple steps that get you reconnected with everyone you may have neglected to stay in touch with over the years. It should be easy for you to talk to the people you already know and have in your database, and if you reconnect with just five people a day, you will start to see results and newfound business in as little as one to two weeks. The key is to systematize the reconnect plan to ensure you reconnect with everyone in your database, and that you do it every day.

If this all sounds too simple, trust me, it is! Now is your moment to make the commitment to change the way you have been doing things. In fact, don't even think of it as change. You are only enhancing what you have been doing by adding the simple E-Myth real estate agent success systems to get the results you really want. If I, a first-generation real estate agent and business owner, can figure this out, I know you can as well. Don't make the change more difficult than it is. Listen to your gut. It's so simple if you allow it to be simple. The not-so-easy part is making the change. I said it was simple, not easy.

You are reading this today for a reason. This is your opportunity to do what took me over twenty years to figure out by implementing the E-Myth principles into my business. In fact, you are taking the shortcut because I am showing you how to implement the E-Myth real estate agent systems without making the mistakes I did. You will most likely still make some, but just ask yourself, "Am I making this more difficult than it needs to be?" I am helping you create the turnkey success system that will give you the opportunity to close one hundred more sales a year without a huge staff.

Let me leave you with one last thought. What if someone offers you $10 million or $100 million for your real estate business? Would your business be worth that? Let's jump back to your BIG DREAM from when you first got into real estate. What was your Big Why? If we did not talk for another five or ten years, and I bumped into you and said, "Hey YOU! How are you? How are things going in your real estate business since you applied *The E-Myth Real Estate Agent* systems?" What would you say? What do you want your real estate business to look like? What do you want your life to look like? Where do you take vacations and with whom? What kind of vehicles do you drive (or fly)? Go BIG! Think BIG, and make changes to get to your BHAG (big hairy audacious goals). Is the way you are currently doing business going to get you there in the next five years? Ten years? Now is your chance to control your future. Make these simple changes and cash in.

Now let's read what Michael has to say about *time*. ❧

On the Subject
of Time

Michael E. Gerber

Money and time are the heaviest burdens of life, and the unhappiest of all mortals are those who have more of either than they know how to use.
—Samuel Johnson

"I'm running out of time!" small business owners often lament. "I've got to learn how to manage my time more carefully!"

Of course, they see no real solution to this problem. They're just worrying the subject to death. Singing the real estate agent's blues.

Some make a real effort to control time. Maybe they go to time management classes or faithfully try to record their activities during every hour of the day.

But it's hopeless. Even when real estate agents work harder, even when they keep precise records of their time, there's always a shortage of it. It's as if they're looking at a square clock in a round universe. Something doesn't fit. The result: the real estate agent is constantly chasing work, money, life.

And the reason is simple. Real estate agents don't see time for what it really is. They think of time with a small "t," rather than Time with a capital "T."

Yet Time is simply another word for your *life*. It's your ultimate asset, your gift at birth—and you can spend it any way you want. Do you know how you want to spend it? Do you have a plan?

How do you deal with Time? Are you even conscious of it? If you are, I bet you are constantly locked into either the future or the past. Relying on either memory or imagination.

Do you recognize these voices? "Once I get through this, I can have a drink . . . go on a vacation . . . retire." "I remember when I was young and practicing real estate was satisfying."

As you go to bed at midnight, are you thinking about waking up at 7:00 a.m. so you can get to the office by 8:00 a.m. so you can go to lunch by noon, because your software people will be there at 1:30 p.m., and you've got a full schedule and a new client scheduled for 2:30 p.m.?

Most of us are prisoners of the future or the past. While pinballing between the two, we miss the richest moments of our life—the present. Trapped forever in memory or imagination, we are strangers to the here and now. Our future is nothing more than an extension of our past, and the present is merely the background.

It's sobering to think that right now each of us is at a precise spot somewhere between the beginning of our Time (our birth) and the end of our Time (our death). No wonder everyone frets about Time. What really terrifies us is that *we're using up our life, and we can't stop it.*

It feels as if we're plummeting toward the end with nothing to break our free fall. Time is out of control! Understandably, this is horrifying, mostly because the real issue is not time with a small "t" but Death with a big "D."

From the depths of our existential anxiety, we try to put Time in a different perspective—all the while pretending we can manage it. We talk about Time as though it were something other than what it is. "Time is money," we announce, as though that explains it.

But what every real estate agent should know is that Time is life. And Time ends! Life ends!

The big, walloping, irresolvable problem is that *we don't know how much Time we have left.*

Do you feel the fear? Do you want to get over it?

Let's look at Time more seriously.

To fully grasp Time with a capital "T," you have to ask the big Question: *How do I wish to spend the rest of my Time?*

Because I can assure you that if you don't ask that big Question with a big "Q," you will forever be assailed by the little questions. You'll shrink the whole of your life to *this time* and *next time* and the *last time*—all the while wondering, *what time is it?*

It's like running around the deck of a sinking ship worrying about where you left the keys to your cabin.

You must accept that you have only so much Time; that you're using up that Time second by precious second. And that your Time, your life, is the most valuable asset you have. Of course, you can use your Time any way you want. But unless you choose to use it as richly, as rewardingly, as excitingly, as intelligently, as *intentionally* as possible, you'll squander it and fail to appreciate it.

Indeed, if you are oblivious to the value of your Time, you'll commit the single greatest sin: You will live your life unconscious of its passing you by.

Until you deal with Time with a capital "T," you'll worry about time with a small "t" until you have no Time—or life—left. Then your Time will be history . . . along with your life.

I can anticipate the question: If Time is the problem, why not just take on fewer clients? Well, that's certainly an option, but probably not necessary. I know a real estate agent with a small company who sees four times as many clients as the average, yet he and his staff don't work long hours. How is it possible?

This real estate agent has a system. By using this expert system, the employees can do everything the real estate agent or his team members would do—everything that isn't real estate agent-dependent.

Be Versus Do

Remember when we all asked, "What do I want to be when I grow up?" It was one of our biggest concerns as children.

Notice that the question isn't, "What do I want to do when I grow up?" It's "What do I want to be?"

Shakespeare wrote, "To be or not to be." Not "To do or not to do."

But when you grow up, people always ask you, "What do you *do?*" How did the question change from *being* to *doing?* How did we miss the critical distinction between the two?

Even as children, we sensed the distinction. The real question we were asking was not what we would end up *doing* when we grew up, but who we would *be*.

We were talking about a *life* choice, not a *work* choice. We instinctively saw it as a matter of how we spend our Time, not what we do in time.

Look to children for guidance. I believe that as children we instinctively saw Time as life and tried to use it wisely. As children, we wanted to make a life choice, not a work choice. As children, we didn't know—or care—that work had to be done on time, on budget.

Until you see Time for what it really is—your life span—you will always ask the wrong question.

Until you embrace the whole of your Time and shape it accordingly, you will never be able to fully appreciate the moment.

Until you fully appreciate every second that comprises Time, you will never be sufficiently motivated to live those seconds fully.

Until you're sufficiently motivated to live those seconds fully, you will never see fit to change the way you are. You will never take the quality and sanctity of Time seriously.

And unless you take the sanctity of Time seriously, you will continue to struggle to catch up with something behind you. Your frustrations will mount as you try to snatch the second that just whisked by.

If you constantly fret about time with a small "t," then Time will blow right past you. And you'll miss the whole point, the real truth about Time: you can't manage it; you never could. You can only *live* it.

And so that leaves you with these questions: How do I live my life? How do I give significance to it? How can I be here now, in this moment?

Once you begin to ask these questions, you'll find yourself moving toward a much fuller, richer life. But if you continue to be caught up in the banal work you do every day, you're never going to find the time to take a deep breath, exhale, and be present in the now.

So let's talk about the subject of *work*. But first, let's read what Brad has to say about *time*. ❧

CHAPTER

22

Find out Where All Your Time is Going

Brad Korn

If your business depends on you, you don't own a business—you have a job.
—Michael E. Gerber, *The E-Myth Revisited: Why Most Small Businesses Don't Work and What to Do About It*

TIME! Do you want more of it? Do you need more of it? What kind of time are we talking about? Time for more work? Time for family? In this chapter I will cover how spending the right amount of time on the right things will get you all the time you want to do what you really want.

No matter what size your real estate business is, I bet you spend most of your time on the things that create frustration and busyness. When you begin to look at your real estate business like a business, you can focus on taking the stress out of your life and enjoy what you are doing.

Remember the 80/20 rule? Eighty percent of what you do every day, including right this minute, is responsible for 20 percent of your

183

income. That means only 20 percent of what you did today was responsible for 80 percent of your income. Remember, no matter what size your team is and no matter how much real estate you sell, this law stands. Once you find the 20 percent that generates 80 percent of your income, and you double those activities into 40 percent of your day, you will double your income! If you are generating $200,000 per year, that means you could go to $400,000 per year . . . or from $500,000 per year to $1 million! I am not even suggesting you spend HALF your day on this strategy. Just 40 percent is all you need to commit to double your income. Use the remaining hours to create the systems that will free up your time.

I know why I struggled with getting control of my time in the beginning, and it is probably the same reason you are struggling. The information I share with you throughout this book is the culmination of more than twenty-five years and upwards of 250 conferences featuring top real estate influencers in the industry. I am not just a conference junkie, I am an implementer. I am sure at this point in the book you realize I have put quite a few systems into place. That is because I created a system for creating systems. It is that system that makes all other systems work at an enhanced level. The key to a successful system is to figure out what the 20 percent is, keep everyone on the team focused on the right activities, and do it every day.

I took the information that works, mastered it, and now help others apply it by sharing what works. I pick things apart, fix what is not getting the results I expected, and streamline the process to spend as little time as possible getting it in place. The purpose of this book is to help you develop your systems faster than I did so you can enjoy the results more quickly and be able to make your real estate business profitable and fun.

Keep Your Eye on the ROI

As a business development specialist, I will share with you what you must do, every day, day in and day out, no matter what to be most efficient, effective and as profitable as you can be. The industry continuously promises to help us make our business as "hands off" as it can. Most data systems today offer follow-up without us having to do much. Turn it on and forget about it. If we get busy, we are taught to hire people to do the things we don't want to do so we can focus on what matters most, like generating more leads. However, do we? Do we generate twice as much new business when we hire someone? Or do we get caught up doing more 80 percent stuff that we like to do?

The industry is full of companies that help with social media so we don't have to spend our time on it—they will do all your posts for you and blast them to multiple platforms. There is a place for services and businesses like these. However, paying for them and putting them into action without a business plan is not how a CEO would run a Fortune 500 company.

I do believe there is value in all these leveraged services, products, and tools. However, new agents desperately trying to survive in their new real estate business have to scrape the bottom of the barrel and borrow money to pay for these services. The result? The agents end up in debt, unable to get their real estate career off the ground long enough to see the return. Or they cancel the service six months to a year later because they have not tracked any sales back to that source. The problem is that the agent didn't create a solid strategy for the return he or she wanted and didn't create a system to automate the plan the day he or she paid for the service.

If anything was truly "hands off" and doubled or tripled an agent's business overnight, don't you think every top agent in the world would be using it? Most companies don't ask agents about their financial situation before signing them up. Why would they? Especially the services that are twenty, thirty or forty dollars per month. Surely that won't put the agent out of business, right?

Those added up for me and SHOULD have put me out of business. I was just not smart enough to get out of real estate when I should have. I often couldn't afford to sign up for the services when I did sign up. When I learned from those mistakes and got smarter about what to sign up for, I would ask for a guaranteed result. The typical response would be, "We can't give any guarantees." The salesman would, however, remind me that it would only take one or two sales to pay for itself, "so give it six months to see if it works for you."

Agents are hungry, and looking for something to get them fast business and closed sales. For example, before you buy a "For Sale by Owner" program. I always suggest first driving around, the good ol' fashioned way, and finding a couple of "for sale by owner" houses. Get one of those sellers to list with you and use that commission to buy the program or system. Have a business plan in place to get the listing before you buy the list of "For Sale by Owners," then when you pay for the list you have a better chance of success. Spend your time on the front end of a plan to get a return on investment on the back end. I bet every one of these services will make you money if you have a plan and system to maximize your results before you start.

In the beginning of one's real estate career, most agents have more time than money. This is not the time to buy your way to success.

The key to success in real estate is getting in front of people. It doesn't have to cost you a lot of money. But it does take time to become top of mind, prepare for the meeting, and go meet them so you can get a contract signed. You will find no long-term, residual benefits without doing the work over and over and over every day. Without a systematized way to do that, you will not have predictable results.

How many twenty- to forty-year real estate veterans do you know who close twelve or twenty-four sales per year? That is one to two closings per month. How much time does it take to close two transactions per month? I say an average of ten hours from the beginning of working with a buyer to the closing. How many hours does it take to sell a listing? Six months can be turned into three to five hours of hands-on work. Yet with only twenty to thirty hours of hands-on work each month, how do they continue to close one or two per month their entire career? The answer is they are running the technician model only. They are busy, but what they are spending their time on during the other hours of the day? Most likely they are not following a business plan or using systems to drive their business.

Everything you do will get you a result if you do it long enough, so the free stuff like open houses or door knocking can make you a lot of commissions if you do it consistently and persistently for a long period of time. If you create a system for those things, the system will make sure you do it regularly and save you time, so you can go get even more business. Again, because agents are just "going with the flow" most of the time, they can find themselves sucked into non-dollar-productive activities. Take, for example a transaction that might not be going smoothly. Agents often get caught up in a "deal" that is blowing up, and it can take all week to keep it together. Refer back to the "Estimating" chapter. Everything can be controlled in your business if you have the right systems. How many minutes does it takes to save a deal? I assure you it does not have to take days.

Deals blow up in my real estate business as well. When I close a property every three days, two or three transactions might blow up in one day. However, because my client fulfillment system is running, and my lead conversion system is running, our phone keeps ringing with more opportunities every day. Meanwhile, the back-end systems help prevent more deals from falling apart, so I don't have to be consumed by them.

There are only three things you should spend all your time on whether you are a new or an experienced agent. *The E-Myth* discusses the three-legged stool of all business: lead generation, lead conversion, and your client fulfillment system. These are the priority items that will generate most of your income through new business plus repeat and referral business. If you spend 40 percent of your day capturing a new lead (and that means getting the address and phone number—not just an email address)—converting the lead by getting them into a two-way conversation, "connecting" with them, creating a customer experience system that blows your clients' socks off every time, and automating the process of the real estate transaction, you will have the opportunity to double your income.

The method I use to create my systems ensures I put everything to the test and tweak those systems until they produce the results I want. There is a strategy and a whole lot of experience (that means doing it wrong over and over and over) behind the things that have doubled and tripled my business. You can avoid some of the mistakes I made by reading this book and implementing systems like the ones I share with you.

What amount of time will it take for you to implement anything, or everything, from this book? How much time and money will you spend going to the next conference you attend? Do have an entire drawer full of ideas on notepads that you can review to see what your next system should be? Do you have a plan from some of the ideas in this book? Have you written them down? I had the same issue. All these great money-making ideas sitting on bookshelves and in drawers in my desk. So I created a system for implementing ideas from a conference. All of that takes time to implement. But with a system for working "ON" my business, I could implement new ideas from conferences once a week. Spending time "ON" my business helped get me where I am today.

We all have the same amount of time every day, and we don't know what day that time is going to stop. While we can't manage "time," we can manage the activities we do during that time.

Here's How to Control Your Time

To get your time under control, you must figure out your 20 percent. Here's what I did early on in my business to accomplish this. Grab a calendar—one of those "week at a glance" calendars. I carried this weekly calendar with me for two weeks. I set an alarm on my phone to go off every thirty minutes. The results will amaze you, and it will become clear where your time is spent. Commit to do this exercise for two weeks. It's not easy, but your commitment over these next two weeks can help you determine what you must focus on, and where your time is going right now.

Here is how the system works. Every time your alarm goes off, grab the calendar and write down what you are doing RIGHT THEN! Don't fluff it. Record whatever it is you are doing at that moment. No judgment or interpretation for the two weeks. When you have done this for two solid weeks, the next step is to evaluate each activity that created income and differentiate between 20 percent activities and 80 percent activities. You will need three different-colored highlighter markers.

After I did this exercise, I was astounded by the results. I used a GREEN highlighter for activities that converted a lead into a client and for getting a commitment from a buyer or seller to do business with me. I highlighted in YELLOW every task I didn't like to do or that I could hire people to do if I could afford it. I used ORANGE for anything I had to do that was not going to make me extra money. For example, my daughter's dance competitions and school events were highlighted in orange. I never missed any of my daughter's events because of work. Let's review the exercise:

1) Green is used for money-generating activities such as, anything involved with getting contact information for new leads. This includes getting a name, address, and phone number. Checking your email to get a new internet lead does not count. Think about it for a second. How many have you converted via email? A lead is not a lead until you can connect and convert, and they are doing business with you. So, what good is a lead if you never get their address and phone number? How many appointments can you set with someone if you never get that information? If you don't get an appointment, you can't convert to a closing. If the activity directly brings new money into your business, it is colored green. Like a Seller signing a listing agreement or a Buyer signing a Buy Agency. Those are "green" activities.

2) Yellow will be used for anything you do every day that could be delegated to someone else. These are the things that you could hire someone to do if you had an extra $10,000 or $20,000 every month. You may not hire out capturing a lead's information, converting the lead at a buyer consultation, or listing an appointment. The items you highlight in yellow would be administrative items,

like organizing a contract, tracking down signatures on amendments, etc. For example, in a real estate transaction, the inspection process is a critical piece. It is part of the client experience. However, it does not involve getting a lead's contact info or converting a new lead to bring in new money. Someone else could do it for you if you had the money to pay a licensed person to get the two-hour inspection started and stay there during the inspection. What if you could just show up at the end, and the inspector took fifteen minutes to show you all the issues that came up? You would have freed up a couple hours of your day, and still accomplished the same result and experience for the client.

3) Orange is used for anything you do every day that only you can do. Like eating dinner with your family. You wouldn't want to hire someone to do that for you, right? Or going to a child's sporting event, play, or going to church. Orange is your "life" stuff.

When I first did this exercise, less than 20 percent of my calendar was GREEN. The rule is simple. If you want to double your bank account, take all the GREEN items and do them twice as much. Again, that would only be 40 percent of your day if you really have 20 percent of your calendar highlighted in GREEN. If you doubled the "green" activities on your calendar right now, how many hours would you spend getting more business? The reality is we don't do enough "green" activities before we get sucked into the tornado of activities that need to be done.

Stay true to this system. Don't color things the wrong color, or you might cheat yourself out of doubling your results. GREEN is only when you get a NEW client to do business with you. Turning in a contract to your office so you can get paid is not a GREEN activity. That should be YELLOW. Getting a buyer to sign a buyer agency and a seller to sign a listing agreement are about the only GREEN things on your calendar. Even going to a listing appointment or conducting a buyer consultation could be YELLOW unless they are signing the contract at that appointment, and you haven't leveraged the listing agent role to another person on your team. Picking up your commission check should be YELLOW. Remember, if money were no object and you could hire as many people as you wanted, YELLOW is an activity someone else could do for you.

This exercise is revealing. You will most likely find that you spend very little time on getting new leads and converting those leads into contracts that will lead to closings. The second step of the process is to automate as many of the yellow things as possible before you hire someone. Set up systems for these items that will automate the process and free up your time. The trick is to replace this newfound time with more "green" stuff. Once you feel like your systems are freeing up your time, and you are doing more green activities and making more money, THEN you can hire help for even more leverage.

As we mentioned in Chapter 8, on "Management," these systems will help you manage your entire real estate client experience and help you hold every team member accountable to deliver the same experience as if you were doing it all yourself. I would challenge you to repeat this process throughout your career. Before you ever hire a person or employee, implement the necessary systems. You will know you have the right systems when you make enough extra profit to put away two to three months of the proposed salary. Once you have done that, then hire! When you have great systems and great people, you will have more time and a lot less stress. Your new hire will be a lot more efficient and get more done when you have proven systems in place.

Now let's read what Michael has to say about *work*. ❖

On the Subject
of Work

Michael E. Gerber

*They intoxicate themselves with work so they won't see how they
really are.*

—Aldous Huxley

In the business world, as the saying goes, the entrepreneur
knows something about everything, the technician knows
everything about something, and the telephone operator just
knows everything.

In a real estate business, real estate agents see their natural work
as the work of the technician. The Supreme Technician. Often to
the exclusion of everything else.

After all, real estate agents get zero preparation working as
managers and spend no time thinking as entrepreneurs—those just
aren't courses offered in today's schools of real estate. By the time
they own their own real estate business, they're just doing it, doing
it, doing it.

At the same time, they want everything—freedom, respect, money. Most of all, they want to rid themselves of meddling bosses and start their own company. That way they can be their own boss and take home all the money. These real estate agents are in the throes of an entrepreneurial seizure.

Real estate agents who have been praised for their ability to handle difficult acquisitions or their extensive knowledge of appraisals believe they have what it takes to run a real estate business. It's not unlike the plumber who becomes a contractor because he's a great plumber. Sure, he may be a great plumber . . . but it doesn't necessarily follow that he knows how to build a company that does this work.

It's the same for a real estate agent. So many of them are surprised to wake up one morning and discover they're nowhere near as equipped for owning their own company as they thought they were.

More than any other subject, work is the cause of obsessive-compulsive behavior by real estate agents.

Work. You've got to do it every single day.

Work. If you fall behind, you'll pay for it.

Work. There's either too much or not enough.

So many real estate agents describe work as what they do when they're busy. Some discriminate between the work they *could* be doing as real estate agents and the work they *should* be doing as real estate agents.

But according to the E-Myth, they're exactly the same thing. The work you *could* do and the work you *should* do as a real estate agent are identical. Let me explain.

Strategic Work Versus Tactical Work

Real estate agents can do only two kinds of work: strategic work and tactical work.

Tactical work is easier to understand, because it's what almost every real estate agent does almost every minute of every hour of every day. It's called getting the job done. It's called doing business.

Tactical work includes filing, billing, answering the telephone, inspecting property, screening sales, handling media advertising services, going to the bank, arranging for financing, and seeing clients.

The E-Myth says that tactical work is all the work real estate agents find themselves doing in a real estate business to *avoid* doing the strategic work.

"I'm too busy," most real estate agents will tell you.

"How come nothing goes right unless I do it myself?" they complain in frustration.

Real estate agents say these things when they're up to their ears in tactical work. But most real estate agents don't understand that if they had done more strategic work, they would have less tactical work to do.

Real estate agents are doing strategic work when they ask the following questions:

- Why am I a real estate agent?
- What will my company look like when it's done?
- What must my company look, act, and feel like in order for it to compete successfully?
- What are the key indicators of my company?

Please note that I said real estate agents ask these questions when they are doing strategic work. I didn't say these are the questions they necessarily answer.

That is the fundamental difference between strategic work and tactical work. Tactical work is all about *answers*: How to do this. How to do that.

Strategic work, in contrast, is all about *questions*: What company are we really in? Why are we in that company? Who specifically is our company determined to serve? When will I sell this company? How and where will this company be doing business when I sell it? And so forth.

Not that strategic questions don't have answers. Real estate agents who commonly ask strategic questions know that once they ask such a question, they're already on their way to *envisioning* the answer. Question and answer are part of a whole. You can't find the right answer until you've asked the right question.

Tactical work is much easier, because the question is always more obvious. In fact, you don't ask the tactical question; the question arises from a result you need to get or a problem you need to solve. Billing a client is tactical work. Advising a client is tactical work. Firing an employee is tactical work. Conducting a property analysis is tactical work.

Tactical work is the stuff you do every day in your company. Strategic work is the stuff you plan to do to create an exceptional company/business/enterprise.

In tactical work, the question comes from *out there* rather than *in here*. The tactical question is about something *outside* of you, whereas the strategic question is about something *inside* of you.

The tactical question is about something you *need* to do, whereas the strategic question is about something you *want* to do. Want versus need.

If tactical work consumes you:

- You are always reacting to something outside of you.
- Your company runs you; you don't run it
- Your employees run you; you don't run them.
- Your life runs you; you don't run your life.

You must understand that the more strategic work you do, the more intentional your decisions, your company, and your life become. *Intention* is the byword of strategic work.

Everything on the outside begins to serve you, to serve your vision, rather than force you to serve it. Everything you *need* to do is congruent with what you want to do. It means you have a vision, an aim, a purpose, a strategy, an *envisioned* result.

Strategic work is the work you do to *design* your company, to design your life.

Tactical work is the work you do to *implement* the design created by strategic work.

Without strategic work, there is no design. Without strategic work, all that's left is keeping busy.

There's only one thing left to do. It's time to *take action*.

But first, let's read what Brad has to say on the subject of *work*. ❧

CHAPTER

24

If I Must Remember to Do It, It Will Not Get Done

Brad Korn

I think that maybe inside any business, there is someone slowly going crazy.
—Michael E. Gerber, *The E-Myth Revisited: Why Most Small Businesses Don't Work and What to Do About It*

Don't assume that if you get too busy, the answer is to hire people. Our industry promotes hiring assistants and buyer agents and anyone else you can hire. It's an incredibly flawed way of handling the situation because your busyness is, in many cases, a short-term state of business. It may only last two to three months, the length of the real estate process from beginning to end. That knee-jerk reaction to hire someone is a year or longer commitment, and the things that are keeping you busy are not.

When you apply the E-Myth principles beyond the technician role and you become a manager and an entrepreneur, you will be able to hold your business accountable. You will be able to hold people accountable for their results and, most importantly, hold yourself accountable for doing what matters most in your business to be successful. Using an entrepreneur's mind-set is thinking of your real estate business like Ray Kroc did with McDonald's.

What systems can you put in place to deliver a consistent, predictable result every time? You may be saying, "Well, Brad, every real estate transaction is different." Sure it is. So is every McDonald's customer, yet Ray Kroc created a system that gets slow people through it as fast as everyone else. The quality of food is predictable. It is the same no matter where you go. Compare that to restaurants where you sometimes have a wonderful meal and other times have a terrible meal. That is not a system for predictable results. McDonald's makes the same meal every time, if everyone on the team follows the system.

Once you complete the calendar tracker exercise I discussed in the last chapter, you will realize that working smarter, for you, means focusing on what grows your business exponentially. There is no reason to settle for the status quo of a business increasing 3 percent or 5 percent per year. You can literally double or triple your business every year. Can you say $10 billion or more sold, like the number of burgers McDonald's has sold? You might say, "I don't want to work that hard." Ray Kroc didn't work that hard. He worked smart by systematizing the results he wanted. If you want to think like Ray Kroc, then implement the principles Michael E. Gerber discusses in the E-Myth books, and apply the turnkey systems I have shared with you throughout this book.

Work Smarter, Not Harder

Let's start off by describing what "working smarter" looks like. During my entire real estate career, I have not seen one service provider or product be the one that every agent signed up for. No one thing brings every agent so much business that everyone in the industry signs up for it, and business dumps in their lap automatically.

I can't even find two or three companies where dozens of the top agents in the world are all clients and are all exploding their business because of that one product or service. I know it doesn't exist because I would sign up for every one of those products or services. Those agents surely would have shared it with me if it worked that well. The day I look on a provider's website and see two dozen testimonials from top real estate agents I recognize, and they have all doubled their business from 300 sales to 600 sales in one year using that system, I will sign up (after I create the strategy and system to get the same results they did).

When you get to "the top," something amazing happens to the sense of camaraderie between agents. So many great agents share everything with each other, and the discussions are generally about having a great life, not necessarily getting the next real estate deal to survive. I surround myself with those people and attribute most, if not all, of my success to everything they shared with me. Many of them are listed in the front of this book.

Working smarter is about building a McDonald's-like franchise system for your real estate process. Not only to deliver the ultimate experience for your client and make the real estate transaction predictable and controllable, but also to help your business grow exponentially! In the early days of my real estate career when I implemented the E-Myth principles, my real estate business doubled every year for several years. I could tell the E-Myth was kicking in when we went from $2 million to $4 million in one year, and then from $4 million to $8 million in sales the next year.

Those systems eventually led to a predictable machine that generates an average of one hundred sales a year, every year, without working harder. I was very fortunate that my business grew on the Missouri side of Kansas City. The lower price point had me producing an extremely high level of transactions to make enough money to support my business and life expenses. I do not get rich on every sale. In fact, I net an average of about $2,000 each time a property closes. Therefore, I needed to sell one hundred homes each year to net the same amount of money an agent in San Diego makes when selling ten homes.

This book is about building the systems that allow me to sell four times more properties than the average full-time real estate agent and ten to twenty times more than the industry average—while putting in fewer hours and getting the most enjoyment possible from life.

The smartest way to work in your business is to stay focused on what brings you new money, new business, and gets it done in the shortest amount of time. That means you are in front of new clients signing buyer agency agreements or listing agreements as many hours of the day as possible. Think about it, what are you spending your day working on? Is it busywork or the things that need to happen to get paid on a contract? Is it getting a brand-new piece of business? To get "smart," you will need systems to process the day-to-day activities. When you create a system that frees you up to get more business without hiring more people, you will begin to experience what "leverage" is about. When you do hire people, your system will make them ten times more efficient, and you can experience growth without working harder.

Good Systems Free You to Focus on Getting Business

The next step is to perfect your systems, so it is YOU that is reflected in the system. When you automate it to the point where you can have anyone work your system and deliver what you deliver, then you have moved to the Ray Kroc model of doing business. Hiring talented people is not the first step. We have already discussed how you are going to find yourself hiring and firing a LOT of people in your career.

You have a 1 percent to 5 percent chance of hiring a "talented" person on one of your first or second hires. That requires luck. Plus, extremely talented people will cost you more than an average person. As Michael Gerber has said, talented people will end up wanting what you want, to take time off to enjoy their family. So when you build a people-driven business backed by talented people, you may not be completely out of the business forever. What happens on the day all of you would rather golf or take a vacation? Or the day they finally realize they could do all this on their own?

That is an incredibly common experience in real estate, and without systems that run the business, it could be devastating to a top agent's business. They could either be out of business one day, working sixty to eighty hours to keep up with the business they created, or—and this is the biggest mistake of all—hire a bunch of people too quickly and deliver a less-than-desirable experience for their clients.

Create systems that will allow you to run your business at an extremely high level by yourself. Then, when you add average people into a system like that, your business will double or triple without more effort on your part. If your systems help them have an enjoyable experience at work every day because the systems are automated, and all they must do is keep them running, you will have experienced what working smarter is about.

Take the calendar we discussed in the last chapter and look for all the "yellow" highlights. That is your focus for systems. Ask yourself, what in this group can be automated in a way that will eliminate time-consuming work and free you up to focus on getting more business? For example, the process of determining value or creating a Comparative Market Analysis (CMA) of a property can sometimes take hours. When I did the calendar exercise, I found that I was spending about 1 to 1½ hours creating an impressive CMA that would persuade the sellers to pick me. That preparation to get the listing was not my 20 percent priority activity. It was when the sellers picked me to work with them.

I created the perfect system for determining value, and now I can do all of that in ten minutes. That one system created the opportunity for me to complete four to five listing appointments in one day. I can physically list twenty-five properties a week, one hundred properties per month and 1,200 properties per year with the systems I created for my business.

Also, all the things that go along with processing a listing are now a system. I call it "the instant listing" system. We can literally have a house on the market, fully marketed, within one hour of the seller signing the listing agreement. The best part is that with this system in operation, we deliver an incredible level of service above and beyond anything I ever did when it took 1½ hours to do the CMA and two weeks to get all the marketing in place for a new listing.

Creating your systems is not difficult if you have a process to follow. I call mine the "Perfect Process System." That's right, a system for your systems. Once again, I have created a simple solution to creating your systems. We discussed why and how to create them in previous chapters. Your "what" to create is the big question, but an obvious one: the systems that are core for your lead capture and lead conversion.

First Find the Right Leads, Then Follow Up

Let's talk about leads for a moment. There are leads you can work that are smarter leads than others, and there are smarter ways to work with all leads. The first category of leads could be anyone in your community who owns a home or wants to buy one. You have specific groups you can market to, such as a neighborhood, your local chamber, or a particular profession, such as doctors. Of course, leads also come in through websites and internet sites. However, studies have shown there is a 1 percent or less chance you will get any business from this group in the short term. Over a long period of time, consistently marketing, you can move it up as high as a 2 percent to 3 percent conversion.

There is another category of leads: the group of people you connect with from today forward. When I say connect, I mean you have a two-way conversation and they don't try to hang up on you. These leads will go on a more consistent follow-up plan. Again, studies show time and time again, once you connect with someone you want to brand yourself as THE real estate expert. This takes a short-term, persistent, repetitive plan to brand you. Branding means when they think of real estate, they think of you right away. An example of a Brand Plan process would be to get something from you every week or a personal touch from you several times throughout the process. Typically, six to nine weeks of touches (studies have shown eight touches in eight weeks) will get you to that branded spot, especially if they are thinking about buying or selling real estate soon. It's important that you mix up the mediums of reaching out. Mail, calls, social media, email, texts, etc. Staying heavier on mail worked for me to ensure they were seeing my name and logo. My touches were light on email, unless that was the only communication method I had or my connection with that individual was very strong.

Once you are branded, realize that more than 98 percent of the people you are staying in touch with will not be buying or selling right now. This group will need a more long-term follow-up to keep you in that branded real estate spot when they think of real estate or someone around them is talking about real estate. Remember, they are not buying or selling right now, so this does not need to be a real estate-only follow-up system. Think about if you had just bought a brand-new car, and you had been by another dealer who kept sending you information about new cars and calling you all the time trying to get you to come in and do a test drive. Eventually you would tell him you just bought a brand-new car and ask him to take you off his list.

All you really need to do is occasionally have something about real estate in your message, but have fun with it too. Talk about life-style in the community, things you are doing, and what is going on in the area. You can even send quotes they might pin up at work. Your name or brand will remind them you are a real estate agent.

Everyone Moves Eventually

We have discussed several times throughout the book that we know everyone will move and approximately 20 percent of them will likely move this year. Because we don't know who the 20 percent are and when they will move, you need to stay top of mind with everyone. The national statistics show that 70 percent to 80 percent of all sellers talk to only one agent before they list their home. You must remain in that No. 1 real estate branded spot to have a 75 percent success rate of getting their listing. If sellers are not calling you to list their home, you are not top of mind.

A few systems for the client fulfillment system will include, but are not limited to, the following:

1) New Seller Prospect to Live Listing Plan
2) New Buyer Prospect to Buyer Agency Signed
3) New Seller Listed until Contract is Received Plan
4) New Buyer Signed Agency Agreement until Contract Accepted Plan
5) Listing Contract Accepted until Contract Closed Plan
6) Buyer Contract Accepted until Contract Closed Plan
7) After Contract Closed Follow-Up Plan

Some additional, more customized plans might include:

1) Investor Follow-Up Plan
2) Credit Repair Follow-Up Plan
3) Foreclosure Hot List Plans
4) Birthday Reminder Plans
5) Property Anniversary Plans
6) Affiliate and Vendor Follow-Up Plans
7) Agent to Agent for Referrals Follow-Up Plan
8) Potential Team Member Follow-Up Plans

You can see why these systems help me stay organized when I have thousands of connections in my contact management system. The system keeps it organized, so my brain doesn't have to. These systems make it feel like I don't have to work hard to sell an average of one hundred properties each year. You can have this too. All you must do is create the systems—and don't make the process more difficult than it really is. I have broken the E-Myth principles down into the absolute simplest, easy process for you. If you keep it simple and implement the systems in each of these chapters, you will find yourself starting to work a lot smarter. Your business will be predictable, and you can enjoy life again. It will be easier to increase your business and build it fast.

Sonya was in a coma for five months. I spent the entire five months at her bedside in the hospital. My business sold ninety-seven homes that year, with only two people running my team. They were both new hires. One new to real estate, and the other had been out of real estate for six or seven years. The system kept our phone ringing with new clients and new business. The two team members didn't know all the systems, but they were doing what every real estate agent does: they were responding to the business that was showing up every day because the system was running.

After my wife passed away, I realized that the only thing that had not happened consistently over that five months was continuing to feed the database. Two months after she passed, our listing inventory had dropped from twenty-five listings to four active listings. I exploded the business back up to thirty-two listings in thirty days just by kicking all the systems into high gear. Those systems allowed me to focus on what matters most and pick up right where the system already was to get more business and grow my listing inventory by almost 700 percent in a very short period.

The next chapter is where the rubber hits the road. It is about putting it all together and implementing.

Work smart; work hard. And, as Michael's about to tell you, *take action!* ❧

On the Subject of Taking Action

Michael E. Gerber

You should know now that a man of knowledge lives by acting, not by thinking about acting, nor by thinking about what he will think when he has finished acting. A man of knowledge chooses a path with heart and follows it.

—Carlos Castaneda, A *Separate Reality*

It's time to get started, time to take action. Time to stop thinking about the old company and start thinking about the new company. It's not a matter of coming up with better companies; it's about reinventing the business of real estate.

And the real estate agent has to take personal responsibility for it. That's you.

So sit up and pay attention!

You, the real estate agent, have to be interested. You cannot abdicate accountability for the business of real estate, the administration of real estate, or the finance of real estate.

Although the goal is to create systems into which real estate agents can plug reasonably competent people—systems that allow the company to run without them—real estate agents must take responsibility for that happening.

I can hear the chorus now: "But we're real estate agents! We shouldn't have to know about this." To that I say: whatever. If you don't give a flip about your company, fine—close your mind to new knowledge and accountability. But if you want to succeed, you'd better step up and take responsibility, and you'd better do it now.

All too often, real estate agents take no responsibility for the business of real estate but instead delegate tasks without any understanding of what it takes to do them, without any interest in what their people are actually doing, without any sense of what it feels like to be at the front desk when a client comes in and has to wait for forty-five minutes, and without any appreciation for the entity that is creating their livelihood.

Real estate agents can open the portals of change in an instant. All you have to do is say, "I don't want to do it that way anymore." Saying it will begin to set you free—even though you don't yet understand what the company will look like after it's been reinvented.

This demands an intentional leap from the known into the unknown. It further demands that you live there—in the unknown—for a while. It means discarding the past, everything you once believed to be true.

Think of it as soaring rather than plunging.

Thought Control

You should now be clear about the need to organize your thoughts first, and then your business. Because the organization of your thoughts is the foundation for the organization of your business.

If we try to organize our business without organizing our thoughts, we fail to attack the problem.

We have seen that organization is not simply time management. Nor is it people management. Nor is it tidying up desks or alphabetizing client files. Organization is first, last, and always cleaning up the mess of our minds.

By learning how to *think* about the practice of real estate, by learning how to *think* about your priorities, and by learning how to think about your life, you'll prepare yourself to do righteous battle with the forces of failure.

Right thinking leads to right action—and now is the time to take action. Because only through action can you translate thoughts into movement in the real world, and, in the process, find fulfillment.

So, first *think* about what you want to do. Then *do* it. Only in this way will you be fulfilled.

How do you put the principles we've discussed in this book to work in your real estate business? To find out, accompany me down the path once more:

1. *Create a story about your company.* Your story should be an idealized version of your real estate business, a vision of what the preeminent real estate agent in your field should be and why. Your story must become the very heart of your company. It must become the spirit that mobilizes it, as well as everyone who walks through the doors. Without this story, your company will be reduced to plain work.

2. *Organize your company so that it breathes life into your story.* Unless your company can faithfully replicate your story in action, it all becomes fiction. In that case, you'd be better off not telling your story at all. And without a story, you'd be better off leaving your company the way it is and just hoping for the best.

Here are some tips for organizing your real estate business:

- Identify the key functions of your company.
- Identify the essential processes that link those functions.
- Identify the results you have determined your company will produce.
- Clearly state in writing how each phase will work.

Take it step by step. Think of your company as a program, a piece of software, a system. It is a collaboration, a collection of processes dynamically interacting with one another.

Of course, your company is also people.

3. *Engage your people in the process.* Why is this the third step rather than the first? Because, contrary to the advice most business experts give you, you must never engage your people in the process until you yourself are clear about what you intend to do.

The need for consensus is a disease of today's addled mind. It's a product of our troubled and confused times. When people don't know what to believe in, they often ask others to tell them. To ask is not to lead but to follow.

The prerequisite of sound leadership is first to know where you wish to go.

And so, "What do I want?" becomes the first question. Not, "What do they want?" In your own company, the vision must first be yours. To follow another's vision is to abdicate your personal accountability, your leadership role, your true power.

In short, the role of leader cannot be delegated or shared. And without leadership, no real estate business will ever succeed.

Despite what you have been told, win-win is a secondary step, not a primary one. The opposite of win-win is not necessarily "they lose."

Let's say "they" can win by choosing a good horse. The best choice will not be made by consensus. "Guys, what horse do you think we should ride?" will always lead to endless and worthless discussions. By the time you're done jawing, the horse will already have left the post.

Before you talk to your people about what you intend to do in your company and why you intend to do it, you need to reach agreement with yourself.

It's important to know (1) exactly what you want, (2) how you intend to proceed, (3) what's important to you and what isn't, and (4) what you want the company to be, and 5) how you want it to get there.

Once you have that agreement, it's critical that you engage your people in a discussion about what you intend to do and why. Be clear—both with yourself and with them.

The Story

The story is paramount because it is your vision. Tell it with passion and conviction. Tell it with precision. Never hurry a great story. Unveil it slowly. Don't mumble or show embarrassment. Never apologize or display false modesty. Look your audience in the eyes and tell your story as though it is the most important one they'll ever hear about business. Your business. The business into which you intend to pour your heart, your soul, your intelligence, your imagination, your time, your money, and your sweaty persistence.

Get into the storytelling zone. Behave as though it means everything to you. Show no equivocation when telling your story.

These tips are important because you're going to tell your story over and over—to clients, to new and old employees, to real estate agents, to team members, and to your family and friends. You're going to tell it at your church or synagogue, to your card-playing or fishing buddies, and to organizations such as Kiwanis, Rotary, YMCA, Hadassah, and Boy Scouts.

There are few moments in your life when telling a great story about a great business is inappropriate.

If it is to be persuasive, you must love your story. Do you think Walt Disney loved his Disneyland story? Or Ray Kroc his McDonald's story? What about Fred Smith at FedEx? Or Debbie Fields at Mrs. Fields Cookies? Or Tom Watson Jr. at IBM?

Do you think these people loved their stories? Do you think others loved (and still love) to hear them? I daresay all successful entrepreneurs have loved the story of their business. Because that's what true entrepreneurs do. They tell stories that come to life in the form of their business.

Remember: A great story never fails. A great story is always a joy to hear.

In summary, you first need to clarify, both for yourself and for your people, the story of your company. Then you need to detail the process your company must go through to make your story become reality.

I call this the business development process. Others call it reengineering, continuous improvement, reinventing your company, or total quality management.

Whatever you call it, you must take three distinct steps to succeed:

- *Innovation.* Continue to find better ways of doing what you do.
- *Quantification.* Once that is achieved, quantify the impact of these improvements on your company.
- *Orchestration.* Once these improvements are verified, orchestrate this better way of running your company so that it becomes your standard, to be repeated time and again.

In this way, the system works—no matter who's using it. And you've built a company that works consistently, predictably, systematically. A company you can depend on to operate exactly as promised, every single time.

Your vision, your people, your process—all linked.

A superior real estate business is a creation of your imagination, a product of your mind. So fire it up and get started! Now let's read what Brad has to say about *taking action.* ✤

CHAPTER

26

The Most Simple Plan; Even You Can Implement

Brad Korn

Freedom does not come automatically; it is achieved. And it is not gained in a single bound; it must be achieved each day. Rollo May
—Michael E. Gerber, *The E-Myth Revisited: Why Most Small Businesses Don't Work and What to Do About It*

While I was writing this book, Michael E. Gerber released another of his top-selling books in the E-Myth series. Nearly thirty years after *The E-Myth* was released, Michael completed one of the most important books of his life, *Beyond the E-Myth: The Evolution of an Enterprise: From a Company of One to a Company of 1,000.* The turnkey systems I am sharing with you in this book will get your business on track to become a profitable and enjoyable business to own and set you up to build a company of 1,000 that doesn't require you to show up.

Once you apply these systems and principles to your current business, you can begin to move toward a balanced business where the Entrepreneur, the Manager and the Technician systems are all working together. If you are truly interested in getting a more consistent, predictable real estate business, don't try and fix what you have now. Don't make the systems in this book more difficult than they really are. Build your new, improved company while your current real estate business is running in the background.

Beyond the E-Myth will help you rediscover the dream, the vision, the purpose, and the mission you had when you first went to real estate school. You may already have lost track of it all because the early stages of the industry do not set you up for success. If you do it right, real estate is the most flexible, lucrative business opportunity with a low barrier of entry that truly allows anyone the opportunity to live their dream, no matter what that dream is. Real estate is your vehicle to make your wildest dreams come true and live the life you deserve.

Do It Now and Every Day

Now is the time. Today is the day. Take action on *The E-Myth Real Estate Agent* principles and systems. Set aside a little time every day to put one more piece into action. Switch your mind-set to focus on why you got into real estate in the first place, and then start building your new real estate business model. Once you have worked on that for a bit, switch gears and go back to your old company for the rest of the day and do whatever you need to do to keep all the plates spinning to make money. Just keep in mind that every day you don't work on your new real estate company, you will continue to stay on the unpredictable roller-coaster.

I recently received a text from a couple I met with in Florida one year ago. At that time, they were at $1 million in sales. They created the core systems they needed to get off the unpredictable roller-coaster ride. I am thrilled to tell you, and not surprised, that they sent me a text one year later that they had just finished at $6 million in sales. That is SIX times more business just by following and implementing these proven systems. If you have a team of agents doing $1 million or $3 million in sales, and you systematize your business to get them all to one hundred sales, you could more than quadruple your results. If you're at $40 million in sales (with a large team), you could jump up to $160 million or more when the team follows the system. You will become a magnet for more real estate agents in your market who haven't figured out *The E-Myth Real Estate Agent* systems.

Trust that I have found the shortest "shortcut" possible and tested it to ensure it is simple to implement and gets results fast. I have been running these systems and models for over twenty years. Understand that I work in these systems every day, and if you read the book *Outliers*, you know it takes about 10,000 hours to reach mastery. I have tallied up the hours I've spent on managing and converting business from a database and the "Make the Phone Ring Again" (MTPRA) systems, and I am well over the 10,000 hours. Just start today! No delay!

Add the five people you met over the last day to your database and write them a note. Do that every day from now on, and watch what happens. You will begin to see your new company take hold within a short period of time. If you need to see results faster, then keep working in your old company doing blast cold calls, knocking on lots of doors, etc. Just keep in mind that will continue to get you short-term results. This is your long-term pipeline plan that will make your phone ring with people wanting to do business with you and refer business to you.

Master the System before Handing It Off

As you build this new company, don't blend your old ways with these new systems. You must understand how all these systems work at a "mastery level" before you hand off anything to a member of your old company team. This is your business. Think of yourself as the owner of a bank, and your database and these systems are your bank vault. You cannot hand over the bank vault combination to every person on your real estate team. What bank owner would give the bank vault combination to everyone in the bank? If you do it yourself, you will not only ensure everything gets in place and stays in place, it will allow you to figure out what your strengths are and what you love to do so you can do those things more and enjoy your new real estate business.

It will also reveal your weak points and where you can systematize the processes to make the system work more easily. Once you've identified the weak spot and worked that part of the system, you can have someone else run the system. Remember, the systems run the business; people just keep the systems going. Once your management system is in place, you can turn over the combination to the vault. Building your "new company" business model is a process, and you are starting with a clean sheet of paper. Design the business you want to have in five years. Design it as though you are already there.

The first system to get you started is a simple one. Remember, I said I have simplified everything to the point you cannot fail unless you continue to do things the way you always have and don't change. You can't create new habits doing things the way you have always done them. The old way won't match your new company.

What is the Fastest Way to Start?

Do you have a database? It may be a list of past clients, your sphere or circle of influence, or maybe even a targeted list of people you market to. Whatever the case, my assumption is you put these people in your database for a reason. You took the time to single out this group of people and put them in a list or database of some sort. Now we're going to convert this list into more than just a database. Let's turn this list into a contact management system. Ninety-nine percent of real estate agents will admit they need to do a better job keeping in touch with their database. The first system for you to implement will do just that. By putting a system in place to reconnect with your current database and feed it new people every day, you will need to have more systems in place as your business grows. A simple plan to start with is to reconnect with your current list of people. They already know who you are, and you know them. I call it the "Reconnect Plan" or "Recharge Your Database" plan. It is only five steps, so it was easy for me to create the system and start the plan on a few people every day.

How did I reconnect with my list of people to start building my business to one hundred sales a year? Here's what my reconnect plan looks like. It can take three to six months to see consistent results from this system. However, dozens of real estate agents have implemented a plan like this and seen one to three transactions in as short as one week.

The Reconnect Plan

1) Send a letter of apology for not staying in touch.
2) Make a reconnection call.
3) Send a handwritten note letting them know how great it was to connect.
4) Send email (to verify that you have the correct address) with the subject line "great connecting last week."

And, like all good plans, the final step is to go on to the next plan.

5) Start the next plan (most likely your Brand Plan).

These plans can be created in the action plans section inside just about every database/contact management system available. The key to success with all these systems is to create a guide or map of your top priority items for the day. When you follow the MTPRA system, this list will be your 20 percent activities that generate 80 percent of your income. When you focus on those items every day, on purpose, and have a system in place to keep you focused, you will begin to see your new real estate dream company emerge.

Do not try to shortcut this process. Stay consistent, stick to the system, and you will get results.

The Letter: Send a letter (snail mail) that says, "It has been a while since we talked, and I apologize. I am going to call you in the next few days." SIGN IT, and only send a few each day. Never try to blast mail or email this letter. It will not be as effective if you do not focus on a small number of individuals at a time.

The Call: This is your opportunity to really connect. You may have so many contacts in your system that when you go through your database, you will want to want to skip over names because you can't remember who they were or if you had a good or bad experience. Stop! Don't skip them! You have them in your database for a reason. Just reconnect. If you try to shortcut this system, it will not work. If you decide to cherry-pick your database, it will snowball until you end up missing 80 percent of your contacts. We only connect with about 20 percent of our "list" naturally and in everyday activities. We lose touch with over 80 percent of them long-term.

Just call. In fact, I challenge you NOT to talk about real estate! The call this time is about them. The script can be a simple as the good 'ol F.O.R.D. system. Talk about them, their Family, Occupation, Recreation (what they do for fun) and Dreams (what they would love to accomplish in their lifetime). Oftentimes, they will ask you how your business is going. Your natural reaction will be to tell them all about you and how excited you are about your business. My suggestion is to not talk about real estate at all. Let them do all the talking. Remember, 98 percent of the people you talk to are not moving right now. If they are, they will tell you.

This conversation will be the basis for your handwritten note. It will help you cross over from just another sales contact to an actual connection with someone who is going to do business with you and/ or send you business in the future. There is only one exception to the "not talk about real estate" rule. If they say "It is so weird that you called today; we are planning to move this week." Then of course you say, "That is why I called!" However, outside of that, whatever you do, do not get caught up in the "So how is real estate going?" question. It's unproductive small talk and typically will not result in a real estate transaction.

The Note: The note is a key piece of the system. The feeling your contacts get when they receive it is the make or break point of how well your continued follow-up and marketing pieces will be received. The note is not about you. It is about them. In fact, try not using the words, "I", "me" or "my" when you write the note. It is about them (Did I say that already?). Also, do not write "PS. If you know anyone thinking about buying or selling real estate, please give them my card." In fact, don't put your card in the note at all. If you really want to make the biggest impact, don't even use a real estate-branded note card. Remember: this note is about them! You'll have plenty of time to get them your logo-branded stuff and your business card and ask for referrals. The reconnect plan is not the appropriate vehicle.

The Email: This is an optional step. However, it helps you clean up the data in your database as you reconnect. If the email address you have for them is old, it may be returned to your inbox as undeliverable. You can get the correct address in your NEXT conversation with them.

The last step in this plan is to start the next plan as soon as this one's complete. Never ever, ever, ever leave this step out. One critical mistake you can make when dealing with a fully automated system is if you don't have to look at it or see it, you can miss mistakes and errors. If you try to keep track of your next touch manually, you are creating too much work for yourself and introducing the possibility of losing touch with that contact again. Everyone you come in contract with from this point forward should be on some type of automated follow-up system, forever.

The trick here is to become masterful at your campaigns and action plans, and set up a series of events for everything you need to remember to do. In the reconnect plan, if you are going to reconnect with five people today, and five more tomorrow, and five more the next day, you will quickly lose track of what day you sent the letter and whom you sent the letter to. And you won't know whom you have to call today. The system will keep track of it all.

Implement the Personal Touch

Stop thinking in bulk! Most real estate agents pull up a long list of people and send one impersonalized thing to them, or they call twenty people a day for several weeks. That is bulk thinking. Your new company is going to move into a one-on-one, relation-ship-based business. This one adjustment in the way you think will change your life and your business.

Whether you are a social person or not, the system is going to keep track of whom you need to be in touch with and how you are going to reach out to them. Your follow-up systems are going to have a lot more personal touches built in to keep you focused on what matters most: the relationship you have with your list of people.

Here are some final words of advice to ensure you get the systems in this book implemented. The first is not to ask other real estate agents what they think about the systems you are imple-menting in your new company. Get advice from them only after they have read the book and implemented these systems them-selves. Your friends and acquaintances will want you to stay status quo with them. They don't want to lose you as an equal, and more than 80 percent of them will not want to do what it takes to get out of the status quo.

Become One of the 3 Percenters

When you get to "the other side," where the successful people hang out, you will see a different world of sharing. In fact, share the information from this book with everyone you know. It is more fun to bring a lot of successful people to the party than to be there by yourself. This is a relationship-based business model that has enough business to go around for everyone you share it with. Chances are, your relationships and database contacts will be mostly different than someone else's. It is a tough process because the 80/20 rule applies to so many things. Only the 20 percenters will have the opportunity to get into the 3 percent club. That means if there are one hundred real estate agents, twenty of them will create a comfortable business. Only three of them will build a big business. The 3 percenters are out on an island by themselves, but it's not a lonely island.

They have chosen to keep moving toward their full potential. When you get there, you will see what it means when someone says, "You are the average of the five people you spend the most time with," a quote attributed to motivational speaker Jim Rohn. Successful people are great people to hang out with, especially when they did what it took to get there, and they come from a mind-set of sharing and working together to achieve more.

The 3 percent club can still have people who are greedy and selfish, but overall the sense of community has been a remarkable experience for me. You get to decide whom you will hang around with. Just about everyone I hang around with in the 3 percent club is generous, sharing, and caring. They love life and are getting much more out of their life. It's not about titles or awards or whom you can beat. It is about camaraderie. It is like getting a gold medal at the Olympics, and now you hang out with all the other gold medalists. You can certainly still hang out with everyone else. I do. I just spend more time with the people who think like I think and don't get stuck in the status quo. Being comfortable and avoiding change is too easy, which is why so many people don't want to do what it takes to get where they really want to be.

You may realize by now that you are not acting like a typical real estate agent in your new company. You are not even in the real estate business anymore. You are in the people and relationship business. You just happen to sell a product and service that pays you very well for what you do. The transaction part of the real estate business is not the critical piece to understand. Knowing your customers and how they are feeling during the transaction is. It is your job to help them have a great experience and feel like they have someone looking out for them when things go wrong.

When you understand what your client's goals are, and you represent them to accomplish that, you will have a lucrative real estate business. You need to understand people and when in their lives it is good for them to buy real estate. When you do, you can leverage yourself and the real estate they own as a vehicle to make THEIR dreams come true. This is when you will experience what *The E-Myth* and *The E-Myth Real Estate Agent* books are sharing with you.

The reality is, you are in the information-gathering business. Your main goal every day is to gather information about everyone you meet because everyone you meet eventually moves. Unless you like putting your nose to the grindstone to find the next real estate deal, the systems in this book will help you build a pipeline of business that will grow exponentially year after year. Your contact management system (or database) will make your phone ring because you created relationships with everyone you met today, yesterday, and even five years ago. When you stay in touch with your relationships in a personalized, systematic fashion, you will cash in on your real estate dreams. As Zig Ziglar said, "If you help enough people get what they want, you will get what you want." ✤

AFTERWORD

Michael E. Gerber

For more than three decades, I've applied the E-Myth principles I've shared with you here to the successful development of thousands of small businesses throughout the world. Many have been real estate agencies—from small companies to large corporations, with real estate agents specializing in markets all over the country.

Few rewards are greater than seeing these E-Myth principles improve the work and lives of so many people. Those rewards include seeing these changes:

- Lack of clarity—clarified
- Lack of organization—organized
- Lack of direction—shaped into a path that is clearly, lovingly, passionately pursued
- Lack of money or money poorly managed—money understood instead of coveted; created instead of chased; wisely spent or invested instead of squandered
- Lack of committed people—transformed into a cohesive community working in harmony toward a common goal; discovering one another and themselves in the process; all the while expanding their understanding, their know-how, their interest, their attention

After working with so many real estate investors, I know that a company can be much more than what most become. I also know that nothing is preventing you from making your company all that it can be. It takes only desire and the perseverance to see it through.

In this book—the next of its kind in the E-Myth Expert series— the E-Myth principles have been complemented and enriched by a story from a real-life real estate agent, such as Brad, who has put these principles to use in his company. Brad had the desire and perseverance to achieve success beyond his wildest dreams. Now you, too, can join his ranks.

I hope this book has helped you clear your vision and set your sights on a very bright future.

To your company and your life, good growing!

ABOUT THE AUTHOR

Michael E. Gerber

Michael E. Gerber is the international legend, author, and thought leader behind the E-Myth series of books, including *The E-Myth Revisited, E-Myth Mastery, The E-Myth Manager, The E-Myth Enterprise, The Most Successful Small Business in the World, Awakening the Entrepreneur Within*, and *Beyond the E-Myth*.

Collectively, Mr. Gerber's books have sold millions of copies worldwide. Michael Gerber is the founder of E-Myth Worldwide, and the co-founder of Michael E. Gerber Companies™, The Dreaming Room™, Design, Build, Launch and Grow™ and the newest venture, Radical U. Since 1977, Mr. Gerber's companies have served the business development needs of over 100,000 business clients in over 145 countries. Regarded by his avid followers as the thought leader of entrepreneurship worldwide, Mr. Gerber has been called by Inc. Magazine, "the world's #1 small business guru." A highly sought-after speaker and strategist, who has single handedly been accountable for the transformation of small business worldwide, Michael lives with his wife, Luz Delia, in Carlsbad, California.

ABOUT THE CO-AUTHOR

Brad Korn

Brad Korn started his real estate career in 1991 while living in Minnesota. His didn't have a very successful start. During first three years in business, Brad says, "I made less than the average agent. I probably should have gotten out of real estate, but I'm glad I didn't." Since that time, Brad has worked in many different capacities within the real estate industry while continuing to sell an average of one hundred properties year after year.

After those first few years, Brad and his team experienced huge growth, several of those years doubling in sales volume. What's the secret? "I am an education sponge," Brad says. He takes time to attend conferences and seminars, and network with other agents; then he implements the plans and ideas. Now Brad and his team are recognized nationally as one of the top real estate teams in the country.

Brad has been featured in two episodes of HGTV's "My House is Worth What?" He continually is in the top 5 percent of real estate agents in his real estate company and local area. He was the winner of a national marketing promotion contest called "Who's Gonna Make It Big?" with HomeStore.com and Realtor.com and presented the grand prize, a five-carat diamond, at the National Association of Realtors® conference in Chicago.

He is one of 200 Top Agents in the world and also a speaker/trainer/panelist for the CyberStars® organization, which is a group of the top tech-oriented real estate professionals who collaborate on ways to use technology to help their clients take advantage of current market conditions and run successful real estate businesses.

Brad has been recognized throughout the real estate industry for his success creating a consistent business. He is a national trainer/ speaker throughout the real estate and mortgage industry. His speaking lead to Brad going through two national coaching certification programs, and coaching and training thousands of agents. He is a founding member of author John Maxwell's coaching team and has been a real estate agent coach and technology coach for several real estate franchises.

Brad has opened a real estate franchise that was profitable the second month it was open. He built that real estate office using the same systems he used in his real estate business. That office had profit every month after that. Brad has been on leadership boards for several real estate organizations and you can find his contributions in national franchise training programs.

In March 2007 Brad was featured in an interview as Howard Brinton's StarPower® Star of the month. He was also featured in the National Association of Realtors®' Realtor Magazine for "Top 10 Most Profitable Websites" and in Real Estate Magazine in an article about "Successful Partners in Marriage and Real Estate." He's been interviewed by sources including Real Estate Performance Systems, CyberStars®, Secrets of Top Selling Agents, NAR Learning Library, Real Estate Rocks webinars, Top Agent Interviews, Masters of Real Estate and Agent Mountain. Brad coached the top mortgage professionals throughout the country as well, and webinars can be found on Maximum Acceleration coaching websites.

ABOUT THE SERIES

The E-Myth Expert series brings Michael E. Gerber's proven E-Myth philosophy to a wide variety of different professional business areas. The E-Myth, short for "Entrepreneurial Myth," is simple: Too many small businesses fail to grow because their leaders think like technicians, not entrepreneurs. Gerber's approach gives small enterprise leaders practical, proven methods that have already helped transform tens of thousands of businesses. Let the E-Myth Expert series boost your professional business today!

Books in the series include:

The E-Myth Attorney
The E-Myth Accountant
The E-Myth Optometrist
The E-Myth Chiropractor
The E-Myth Financial Advisor
The E-Myth Landscape Contractor
The E-Myth Architect
The E-Myth Real Estate Brokerage
The E-Myth Insurance Store
The E-Myth Dentist
The E-Myth Nutritionist
The E-Myth Bookkeeper
The E-Myth Veterinarian
The E-Myth Real Estate Investor
The E-Myth Chief Financial Officer
The E-Myth Real Estate Agent

Forthcoming books in the series include:

The E-Myth HVAC Contractor
The E-Myth Plumber
. . . and 300 more industries and professions

Have you created an E-Myth enterprise? Would you like to become a Co-Author of an E-Myth book in your industry? Go to www.MichaelEGerberCompanies.com

THE MICHAEL E. GERBER
ENTREPRENEUR'S LIBRARY
It Keeps Growing . . .

Thank you for reading another E-Myth Vertical book.

Who do you know who is an expert in their industry?

Who has applied the E-Myth to the improvement of their
practice as Brad Korn has?

Who can add immense value to others in his or her industry
by sharing what he or she has learned?

Please share this book with that individual and share that individual with us.

We at Michael E. Gerber Companies are determined to transform the state
of small business and entrepreneurship worldwide. *You can help.*

To find out more, email us at Michael E. Gerber Partners, at
Partners@michaelegerber.com

To find out how *YOU* can apply the E-Myth to *YOUR* practice,
contact us at gerber@michaelegerber.com

Every Life a Legacy! Every Small Business a School! - Michael E. Gerber

---

Michael E. Gerber, Co-Founder | Chairman
Michael E. Gerber Companies™
Creator of The E-Myth Evolution™
P.O. Box 130384, Carlsbad, CA 92013
760-752-1812 O • 760-752-9926 F
gerber@michaelegerber.com
www.MichaelEGerberCompanies.com

Join The Evolution^{SM}

Find the latest updates:
www.MichaelEGerberCompanies.com

New Program:
www.RadicalU.com

Watch the latest videos:
www.youtube.com/michaelegerber

Connect on LinkedIn:
www.linkedin.com/in/michaelegerber

Connect on Facebook:
www.facebook.com/MichaelEGerberCo

Connect on Instagram:
www.instagram.com/michaelegerber

Follow on Twitter:
http://twitter.com/michaelegerber

THE MICHAEL E. GERBER
Beyond the E-Myth
LIBRARY

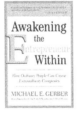

CPSIA information can be obtained
at www.ICGtesting.com
Printed in the USA
BVHW032225090321
602113BV00022B/2272/J

9 781618 350435